Catfishing Strategies

MINNETONKA, MINNESOTA

Editor Dick Sternberg has fished across North America, combining those skills with his training in biology and love of words, to create over twenty books on fishing. This is a catfish book from a "river rat" at heart.

Catfishing Strategies

Mike Vail
Vice President,
Products and Business Development

Tom Carpenter
Director of Book and New Media Development

Dan Kennedy
Book Production Manager

Michele Teigen
Book Development Coordinator

Julie Cisler, Dave Schelitzche
Book Design & Production

Gina Germ
Photo Editor

Bill Lindner Photography (Bill Lindner, Tom Heck, Brook Martin, Jason Lund and Pete Cozad)
Dick Sternberg
Jeff Samsel
Dan Gapen
Minnesota Historical Society, *page 7*
Virginia Tourism Corporation
© GMCO Maps and Charts pp. 128, 129
Grady Allen
Bill Vanderford
Mark Emery
Don Wirth
Steve Pennaz
Keith Sutton
Jim Niemiec
Stephen Davis
Photography

Chris Altman
Dan Gapen
Jim Niemiec
Jeff Samsel
Dick Sternberg
Keith Sutton
Don Wirth
Contributing Writers

Kim Graham, Missouri Department of Conservation
Donald C. Jackson, Mississippi State University
Wayne Hubert, Wyoming Cooperative Fish & Wildlife Research Unit
Biological Consultants

Dave Schelitzche
Joe Tommelleri
David Rottinghaus
Illustration

Bruce Holt
Julie Lindemann
Proofreading

A special thanks to our catfish recipe contributors:
Lee Brown—Farris, OK
Julio Prieto—Riverton, UT
Thomas Schaad—Leawood, KS
Mrs. James E. Ray Sr.—Morton, MS
Vince Pugliese—Pittsburgh, PA
Duane R. Bowers—Dillon, SC
Julius Gonzalez—Bayonne, NJ
Gary A. Crim—Bessemer, AL
Dorothea Ledford—Columbus, GA
Brenda Cardwell—Stockton, CA
Tammie McElroy—Ringdale, AR
John Schumacher—New Prague, MN
Teresa Marrone—Minneapolis, MN

9 8 7 6 5 4 3 2 1

ISBN 1-58159-012-1

North American Fishing Club
12301 Whitewater Drive
Minnetonka, MN 55343

CONTENTS

INTRODUCTION

America's freshwater fishing scene has changed in subtle yet significant ways over the past 50 years. We tend to put the spotlight on a certain species and then, after a honeymoon period, move on to another species.

The 50s, 60s and 70s, for example, were the golden age of bass fishing. Fertile reservoirs supported phenomenal bass fisheries and anglers hungered for knowledge on how to catch these fish.

The 80s and 90s became the age of the walleye, as tournaments resulted in an explosion of walleye fishing knowledge.

Now it's the catfishes' turn.

Catfish have long been one of our nation's most popular gamefish, but catfish anglers found it difficult to learn much about their favorite fish. Those days are over.

Catfishing Strategies, edited by former fisheries biologist and angling expert Dick Sternberg, is one of the most complete catfish titles ever produced. *Catfishing Strategies* is the book for which catfishermen have waited years.

What an exciting time to be a catfisherman!

Steve Pennaz

Executive Director
North American Fishing Club

UNDERSTANDING CATFISH

*T*he first step to consistent catfishing success is knowing your quarry.

CATFISH:
THE ALL-AMERICAN GAMEFISH

For centuries, catfish have reigned as king of North American waters.

Long before recorded history, American Indians pursued these bewhiskered fish as an important part of their diet. Archaeological explorations of ancient Indian villages have revealed scores of catfish ear bones, or otoliths, buried in their trash heaps.

Indians hunted catfish primarily for their tasty flesh, but the sturdy dorsal and pectoral spines of the fish were also used as needles and awls.

Indians developed many of our most effective catfishing techniques. They attached hooks fashioned from bone to long lines of hemp, hair or sinew, which were stretched across a stream. Today, we call such rigs "trotlines." Often, a single hook would be tied to a short piece of line and then suspended from a green tree limb above a riverbank. These rigs are now called "limblines" or "bush-hooks."

Indians were aware of the catfish's extraordinary senses of smell and taste. One unique method for capturing catfish was practiced by the Choctaw tribes in what is now Mississippi and Alabama. A cylindrical trap baited with a fresh, bloody animal was dropped into the

Commercial catfishing was once a booming industry. Now, sportfishing gets all the focus!

water. Blood seeping into the water would then attract catfish and, when the fisherman saw a catfish enter the trap, he would quickly pull a string and the fish was caught.

Europeans migrating to this country quickly discovered the catfish, and it soon became one of the most desired table fish. By the 1830s, commercial catfishing in the big rivers of the South was a booming industry. Channel, blue and flathead catfish pulled from the depths of the Mississippi, Missouri and Ohio rivers were sold in local fish markets and shipped to nearby areas. Catfishing was a respected profession.

Today, catfishing rivals bass and panfish fishing in popularity among anglers, and it's easy to understand why:
- Fish connoisseurs will tell you that few other fish

have such delicate, mild-tasting flesh.
- Although cats don't display the aerial acrobatics of a smallmouth bass or rainbow trout, they fight with a raw, brutal strength that would put virtually any of the more glamorous gamefish to shame.
- Catfish are widespread and, where they are found, are usually quite numerous.
- Catfish are ravenous feeders, often providing the angler with nonstop action.
- Some catfish species grow to enormous sizes, offering anglers the chance to do battle with a fish weighing more than 50 pounds—perhaps even twice that.

On the following pages, we will acquaint you with all of North America's catfish species and show you how they differ.

CHANNEL CATFISH

(Ictalurus punctatus)

Like all other North American catfish, the channel cat is a member of the Ictaluridae family. Ictalurids possess four pairs of barbels; a fleshy adipose fin (small fin on back); smooth, scale-free skin; and bony spines in front of the dorsal and pectoral fins. Zoologists have identified 37 Ictalurid species in North America. Besides channel catfish, the species most popular among anglers include blue, flathead and white catfish. Many fishermen also pursue black, brown and yellow bullheads.

Description

Channel cats resemble blue cats; in fact, they're often called "blue channel cats." The sides are bluish to greenish gray with a silvery tinge. As channel cats age, they turn a slate blue color, much like that of the blue catfish.

Juvenile channel cats (called fiddlers) and small adults usually have numerous black spots. In fact, the channel cat's Latin name, "punctatus," means "spotted." But the spots normally disappear in older, larger individuals.

Female channel cats have narrower heads and slimmer shoulders than males. Females also sport lighter colors and more rounded bodies.

Habitat & Range

The channel cat is the most adaptable of North America's big catfish. It is more tolerant of turbidity than its cousins, and can survive in most any unpolluted warmwater environment.

Channel cats thrive in medium- to large-size rivers with slow to moderate current, but they are also found in shallow to mid-depth reservoirs and in small lakes and ponds. Channels will not tolerate as much current as blue cats. They prefer a clean sand, gravel or rubble bottom with an abundance of cover such as log jams, wing dams or brush piles. They're commonly found in tailrace areas where there is an abundance of food.

The native range of the channel catfish extends from the Appalachian Mountains west to the Rockies, and from the Hudson Bay drainage south to the Gulf of Mexico. Their preferred temperature range, 75 to 80°F, is slightly lower than that of flatheads and blues, explaining why their native range extends far-

Channel catfish range.

ther north. Channel cats have been widely stocked in the United States, particularly in western reservoirs.

Habits

Channel cats spawn in late spring, usually at water temperatures in the 70 to 75°F range. Like other cats, they're difficult to find at spawning time. They build their nests in dark, secluded spots such as holes in the bank, sunken barrels or alongside boulders or logs. Males protect the nest until the young disperse.

During the spawning season, males typically assume a dark blue-black color and their heads become knobby and swollen while the lips thicken and look somewhat fleshy.

Of all the catfish species, channels have the least selective food habits. They will take live fish as well as dead or rotting ones, and will also eat larval aquatic insects, terrestrial insects, crayfish, crabs, snails and clams. Channel cats tend to consume more fish as they grow older, and they reach the largest size in waters where fish make up the bulk of their diet.

Like blue cats, channel cats have a deeply forked tail. But the anal fin of a channel is shorter than that of a blue. It has 24 to 29 rays (cartilaginous spines) while a blue's has 30 to 36. The bottom edge of a channel cat's anal fin is also more rounded.

Channel cats may feed at any time of the day or night, but veteran catfishermen know that feeding is heaviest after sundown. Channels are also known for their habit of gorging themselves when the water starts to rise. They feed very little at water temperatures below 50°F.

Age & Growth

Channel cats have been known to live more than 20 years, but the usual life span is 10 years or less.

In the North, it takes 7 to 9 years for a channel cat to reach 3 pounds. In the South, they reach that size in only 4 or 5 years.

Most channel cats taken by anglers range from 1 to 10 pounds, with 2- to 4-pounders being most common. As is true with most catfish, male and female channel cats grow to roughly the same size.

Sporting Qualities

Willing biters, channel cats respond to "stinkbaits" better than flatheads or blues. They can also be attracted by chumming, usually with rotten cheese or fermented grain. In addition, channels can be taken on dried blood, chicken liver, worms, minnows and even artificial lures such as jigs and spinners.

Once hooked, a channel cat wages a strong, determined battle in deep water.

Channel catfish.

World Record

The all-tackle world-record channel cat is W.B. Whaley's 58-pound giant taken from South Carolina's Santee-Cooper Reservoir system on July 7, 1964. Because large channel cats resemble blue cats, it is quite possible that larger specimens have been caught but were not reported because they were assumed to be blues.

Holes in the bank afford catfish protection around spawning time.

"Fiddlers" have numerous small, black spots on their sides.

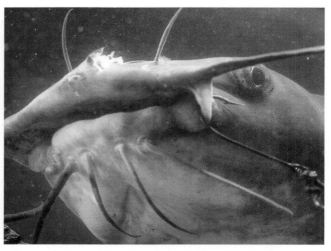

Channel cats, particularly large males, have an upper jaw that protrudes well past the lower.

FLATHEAD CATFISH

(Pylodictis olivaris)

The flathead is North America's second-largest catfish, exceeded in size by only the blue cat. This unusual looking cat is easy to distinguish from other members of the catfish family.

The flathead is the only North American catfish species with a squarish tail and protruding lower jaw; the others have forked tails and underslung lower jaws. The anal fin is short, with 14 to 17 rays.

Description

As its name suggests, the flathead has a broad, flattened forehead. The back and sides are light brown with darker brown or black mottling, which may not be present in fish from highly turbid water. The belly ranges from pale yellow to creamy white. The tiny eyes

Flathead catfish.

help give the fish a distinctive look.

Common names for the flathead include the mud cat, yellow cat, Appaloosa cat, shovelhead cat and Johnnie cat.

Habitat & Range

Flatheads inhabit large river systems, including any impoundments and major tributaries. Although they are commonly called mud cats, they seldom frequent areas with a soft bottom. River-dwelling flatheads spend most of their time in large, sluggish pools with a sandy or gravelly bottom or in the food-rich tailwaters of dams. In impoundments, you'll often find flatheads around flooded timber, stumps or tangles of woody cover.

Flatheads prefer water temperatures in the upper 70s to low 80s and can tolerate temperatures of more than 90°F. Contrary to popular belief, they are not able to survive in highly polluted waters or in waters with extremely low dissolved-oxygen levels.

In the North, flatheads begin moving into traditional wintering holes in late fall. Thousands of cats congregate

Flathead catfish range.

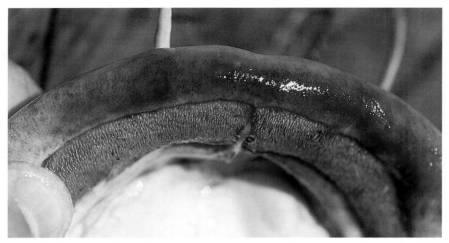

A pad of recurved teeth on the upper jaw make it virtually impossible for a fish to break free once a flathead closes its jaws.

in a few acres of water, usually where there is an abundance of woody cover to break the current. They spend the winter in a state of near dormancy, lying flat to the bottom and allowing a layer of silt to accumulate on their backs. They remain in these wintering holes until the water begins to warm in spring.

Habits

An extremely efficient predator, the flathead has broad, powerful jaws with a large pad of tiny recurved teeth on the upper jaw that makes it virtually impossible for prey to escape once the fish clamps down on it.

Flatheads have been observed holding quietly on the bottom with their enormous mouths wide open, waiting for a smaller, hapless fish to investigate the curious cavity.

The flathead's diet consists mainly of live fish, but it also eats crayfish and clams. Unlike channel catfish, flatheads rarely consume rotten food. This explains why fishermen use fresh, lively bait-

fish such as suckers, carp, large shiners and sunfish, or fresh cut bait, rather than the "stinkbaits" and other prepared baits that work so well for channel cats. It's not unusual for an angler pursuing big flatheads to bait up with a 2-pound carp or sucker.

Flatheads are secretive, solitary fish. They feed mainly at night, moving from the security of woody cover in a deep pool to forage in a shallow riffle area. After feeding, an adult flathead returns to its favorite resting spot where it remains until the next night unless it is disturbed. So it's easy to see why the best flathead anglers are night stalkers.

Flatheads spawn in late spring or early summer, a little later than channel cats. Spawning usually takes place with water temperatures in the low to upper 70s. The fish often spawn in a natural hole in the bank, but they may excavate nests near logs or boulders. "Noodlers" take advantage of the flathead's spawning habits by reaching into holes in the bank and grabbing fish that may exceed

70 pounds. Many noodlers have missing fingers—real proof of the power of the flathead's jaws.

Age & Growth

It's not unusual for flatheads to live 15 years, and some individuals probably live much longer. In the North, a 15-year-old flathead averages about 30 pounds; in the South, more than 50.

Five- to 10-pound flatheads are most commonly caught by anglers, and 30- to 40-pound fish rarely warrant a mention in a hometown newspaper.

Sporting Qualities

One of the strongest fighting freshwater fish, flatheads typically wage a dogged battle in deep water. You struggle for ten minutes to pull the fish up a few feet, then it retreats to the bottom and you start all over. It's not surprising that serious mudcatters use pool-cue rods and 50-pound line. In much of the South, jug fishing, trotlining and noodling account for more flatheads than does rod-and-reel fishing.

Flatheads taken from clean water have firm, flaky, white meat with an excellent flavor.

World Record

The world-record flathead, a 92 pounder, was taken by Robert E. Pardee in Toledo Bend Lake, Texas, on February 25, 1995. There have been numerous undocumented reports of flatheads weighing more than 100 pounds, and at this printing a 123-pound giant is pending as the new world record.

Flatheads vary greatly in coloration. Some are nearly black while others (shown) have a bright yellowish hue.

BLUE CATFISH
(Ictalurus furcatus)

Blue cats are the largest North American catfish species. In the mid-1800s, when commercial catfishing was a booming industry along the Mississippi River, gigantic blue cats reportedly hung like sides of beef in local fish markets. Blues no doubt reached weights approaching 200 pounds in those times, and 100 pounders are still taken occasionally.

Description

As their name suggests, these fish are bluish to grayish in color, although some individuals are silvery, accounting for the name "silver cat."

Blues are somewhat stockier than channels and their head is smaller compared to the rest of their body.

The profile, from the dorsal fin forward, is straight and steeply sloped, giving the body a distinctive, wedge-shaped appearance.

Habitat & Range

Blue cats are big-river fish, thriving in mainstem rivers and their major tributaries. Blues favor faster, clearer water than channel cats and are usually found over a clean sand, gravel or rubble bottom.

Blue catfish prefer water temperatures in the 77 to 82°F range, slightly higher than the range of channel cats. Like channels, blues are often found in tailrace areas where food is abundant.

Blue catfish are native to the Mississippi, Missouri and Ohio river drainages in the central and southern states, and their range extends south into Mexico and northern Guatemala. Blues have been stocked in many reservoirs in both the eastern and western U.S., where they commonly grow to enormous sizes. In some impoundments, however, biologists believe that these fish fail to reproduce.

Unfortunately, America's blue catfish population has declined since 1900. Dam and lock construction along big rivers has blocked spawning runs, limiting the numbers of blues in many sections of the larger rivers. And by impounding the water, dams take away the current that blues prefer.

Habits

Blues tend to be more pelagic (open-water oriented) than other cats. They roam widely, often in large

Blue catfish range.

schools, foraging at any depth. Many commercial anglers report catching more blues on trotlines that are suspended under the surface than on lines fished on the bottom.

Biologists consider blue cats "opportunistic" feeders, because they will eat whatever food is available. Although fish are the primary food of adult blues, they will also take insects, crayfish and clams. Large blues do not hesitate to swallow fish weighing several pounds. In many southern reservoirs and rivers, the diet of blue catfish consists almost entirely of gizzard and threadfin shad.

Blue cats feed at any time of the day or night and, unlike other catfish species, they continue to feed heavily even when water temperatures dip into the 40s.

Blues are more migratory than other catfish species. During the pre-spawn period they often migrate upriver, congregating in enormous schools below dams that block their spawning run. But as winter approaches, they generally move down-river.

Blues, like channel cats, have a deeply forked tail. But unlike channels, their sides are not spotted (even on small fish) and their anal fin is considerably longer (30 to 36 rays), with a straighter bottom edge.

Spawning takes place in late spring or early summer, usually at water temperatures from 70 to 75°F. Blues, like channels, nest in some type of cavity that provides shade and protection from predators. Common spawning sites include undercut banks, root wads, depressions in the bottom and sheltered areas behind boulders.

Age & Growth

Blues are longer-lived than other catfish; the largest specimens are usually more than 20 years old.

Growth varies greatly in different bodies of water, depending on forage availability. In the Louisiana Delta, for example, blues grow to 33 inches (about 17 pounds) in only 6 years. In Lake

Blue catfish.

Chickamauga, Tennessee, they reach only 1.2 pounds in the same amount of time.

Most blue catfish taken by today's anglers are in the 3- to 15-pound range.

Sporting Qualities

Blue cats offer anglers something that few other freshwater gamefish can: the possibility of catching a 100-pound-plus fish.

In the 1800s, blues evidently reached much larger sizes. In his book *Steamboating Sixty-Five Years on Missouri's Rivers*, William Heckman reported, "... the largest known fish ever caught in the Missouri River was taken just below Portland. This fish, caught in 1866, was a blue channel cat and weighed 315 pounds."

Blues will take a variety of live baits, cut baits and prepared baits. In addition to hook-and-line fishing, blues are commonly taken by jug fishing, trotlining and noodling.

But commercial fishing has taken its toll on the largest blues. Some states are now taking steps to reduce commercial harvest so that more trophy blues are available to sport fishermen.

Blue cats are considered excellent eating; they have white, flaky, mild-tasting meat.

World Record

William P. McKinley holds the world record with a 111-pound blue catfish taken on July 5, 1996, in Wheeler Reservoir, Alabama. Several other 100-pound-plus blues have been caught and officially weighed since, and a 112-pounder is now being submitted for consideration as the new record.

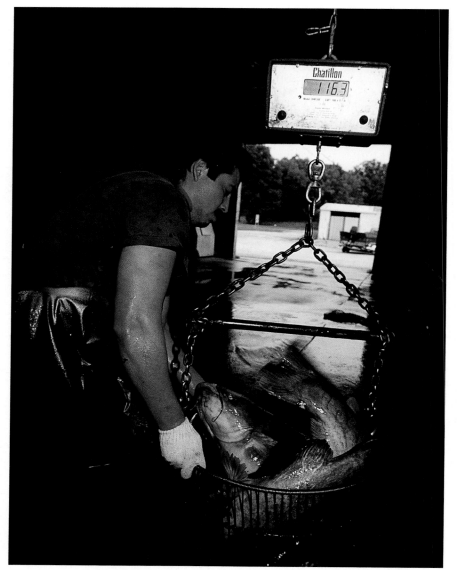

Trotlining and other types of commercial fishing have greatly reduced numbers of giant blue catfish.

A blue cat (left) can be distinguished from a channel (right) by its longer anal fin and wedge-shaped body.

WHITE CATFISH
(Ameiurus catus)

Even ardent catfish anglers may not be familiar with these small catfish because their native range is so limited. And where they coexist with channel cats, anglers often fail to make the distinction. But white catfish are gaining in popularity as stocking expands their range. They are especially popular in "fee-fishing" ponds.

Description

White catfish bear a close resemblance to channel cats, but they do not grow nearly as large. Whites often possess the greenish-silver or bluish-silver coloration of the channel cat, but there is usually a sharper demarcation between the darker color of the sides and the whitish belly. Some whites are mottled with milky, pale gray to dark blue splotches.

Habitat & Range

White catfish prefer slow current and are commonly found in sluggish streams, marshes, bayous, river backwaters, ponds and reservoirs.

Compared to other catfish species, they are more tolerant of a soft, silty bottom and high water temperatures. Their preferred temperature range is 80 to 85°F. White cats can also tolerate more salinity than other catfish species, so they are often found in the lower reaches of coastal rivers where other cats are absent.

The white catfish is sometimes called the "Potomac cat" because it was once limited to the Atlantic coastal

White catfish.

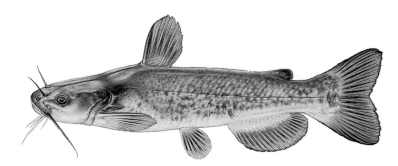

The tail of a white cat is not quite as deeply forked as that of a channel, the body is never spotted, the anal fin is shorter (19 to 23 rays) and the chin barbels are white rather than black or brown.

White catfish range.

states—from Chesapeake Bay to Florida—and a few of the gulf states. Whites have been successfully introduced into many waters in California and Nevada, as well as into numerous fee-fishing lakes across the country.

Habits

White catfish are gluttonous feeders. Although small fish are their favorite food item, they will also take fish eggs, aquatic insects, crustaceans and even pondweeds.

Although white catfish may feed at night, they are not as nocturnal as the other catfish species.

Like other catfish, white cats spawn in late spring or early summer, generally at water temperatures in the 70 to 75°F range. They build a large nest, usually on a sand-bar, and the male guards the eggs and fry.

Age & Growth

White catfish may live up to 14 years but their growth rate is the slowest of all the catfish species. In the northern part of their range, it takes from 9 to 11 years for a

The white cat is a willing biter at any time of the day.

white cat to reach 2 pounds. In the southern part, they normally reach that size in 6 or 7 years. The majority of white cats caught by anglers weigh from 1 to 3 pounds.

Sporting Qualities

The white cat's willingness to take most any kind of bait, combined with its tendency toward daytime feeding, explains why it is so popular in fee-fishing lakes and ponds.

Whites are scrappy fighters but their relatively small size limits their popularity in regions where anglers have access to bigger cats.

An excellent table fish, the white catfish has firm, white flesh.

World Record

The world-record white catfish, a 22-pounder, was caught on March 21, 1994, by James Robinson in William Land Park Pond, California.

BLACK BULLHEAD
(Ameiurus melas)

Black bullheads are the most common bullhead species and are often so abundant that they become stunted. Where stunting is not a problem, however, they grow to respectable size. In fact, the world record for the black bullhead is larger than that of any other bullhead species.

Often the dominant species in freeze-out lakes, black bullheads can tolerate dissolved-oxygen levels lower than any other fresh-water gamefish with the

Black bullheads have pectoral spines with tiny barbs that don't catch on your thumb and finger when you run them along it.

Weakly barbed pectoral spine

Black bullhead range.

possible exception of the yellow bullhead (p.21). Black bullheads are most abundant in lakes and streams with turbid water, a muddy bottom and very little current. They favor water temperatures in the 75 to 85°F range.

Black bullheads spawn in late spring or early summer at water temperatures in the upper 60s. The female builds a nest in weedy or woody cover and, after spawning, helps the male guard the eggs and young. After the young leave the nest, they can often be seen swimming along the shoreline in tight schools.

The black bullhead's diet consists of a wide variety of foods including small fish, fish eggs, worms, leeches, mollusks, insects and plant material.

Although black bullheads live up to 10 years, their growth rate is highly variable, depending on whether or not the population is stunted. If stunting is not a problem, a black bullhead in the North usually reaches a weight of 1 pound in 7 to 9 years; in the South, only 4 or 5 years.

Black bullheads are not fussy; you can catch them on most any bait including worms, cheesebait, stinkbait liver and even chunks of soap.

Even though black bullheads are weak fighters, their tasty white meat makes them popular with many anglers.

The world record black bullhead, an 8-pound, 15 ouncer, was caught by Charles M. Taylor in Sturgis Pond, Michigan, on July 19, 1987.

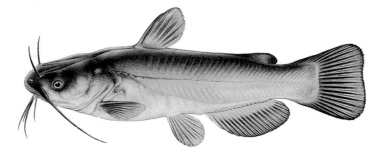

Black bullheads have dark greenish to goldish sides and dark-colored barbels. They are sometimes confused with brown bullheads (p. 20), but the tail is slightly notched, there is a pale, crescent-shaped bar at the base of the tail and their pectoral spines are not as strongly barbed (above).

Brown bullhead range.

tures in the upper 70s or low 80s.

Spawning takes place in late spring or early summer, generally at water temperatures in the low 70s. Both parents build a nest on a mud or sand bottom, usually among roots, logs or other cover that provides shade. After spawning they continue to guard the nest and protect the young.

The diet of a brown bullhead is similar to that of a black, consisting of small fish, fish eggs, worms, leeches, mollusks, crayfish, insects and plant material.

Brown bullheads may live up to 12 years, but the usual life span is much shorter. In the northern part of the range, it takes 7 or 8 years to grow a 1-pounder; in the southern part, only 4 or 5 years.

Although brown bullheads are not strong fighters, they'll give you a little more tussle than a black. Their meat is reddish or pinkish, rather than white, but it is quite firm and has a good flavor.

The world-record brown bullhead weighed 6 pounds, 2 ounces. It was caught by Bobby L. Gibson, Jr., in the Pearl River, Mississippi, on January 19, 1991.

Brown bullheads have a strongly-barbed pectoral spine (inset) that catches your thumb and finger when you run them along it.

BROWN BULLHEAD
(Ameiurus nebulosus)

Brown bullheads are usually found in larger, deeper lakes than other bullhead species. They also thrive in some smaller lakes and ponds, and in slow-moving streams, but they are not as resistant to freeze-out as black bullheads. Brown bullheads favor water tempera-

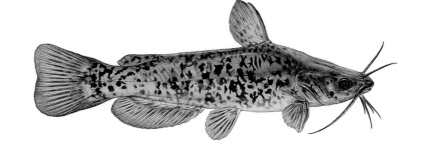

Brown bullheads usually have mottled sides and a tail that is square or has only a very slight notch. The pectoral spines are longer and more sharply barbed than those of a black bullhead and there is no pale crescent-shaped mark at the base of the tail.

YELLOW BULLHEAD

(Ameiurus natalis)

Yellow bullhead.

Although bullheads are usually considered a muddy-water fish, yellow bullheads prefer clear water with a heavy growth of aquatic vegetation. But they can tolerate polluted water and extremely low dissolved-oxygen levels.

Yellow bullheads thrive in warm, slow-moving streams; ponds; small, weedy lakes and weedy bays of larger lakes. Their preferred temperature range is 75 to 80°F.

The yellow bullhead's diet is not much different from that of other bullheads, but they're known for their habit of scavenging most any kind of organic matter off the bottom. They will eat bits of weeds, aquatic insects and other invertebrates and, on occasion, live fish.

Spawning takes place in late spring or early summer, when the water temperature warms to the upper 60s or low 70s. The fish may nest in a cavity in the bank or dig out a depression in a clean bottom. When spawning has been completed, the male guards the nest until the eggs hatch and the fry disperse. Yellows have a lower reproductive rate than blacks, meaning that they're less prone to stunting.

Yellow bullheads grow more rapidly than blacks or browns, but their life span seldom exceeds 7 years. There is little difference in growth rate from north to south. It takes about 5 years to grow a 1 pounder in the northern part of the range and about 4 years in the southern part.

Although yellow bullheads do not put up a strong fight, they are willing biters and, when taken from cool water, are good eating. Effective baits include worms, leeches, crickets, grubs, cut bait, doughballs, stinkbait and cheesebait.

The largest yellow bullhead on record weighed 4 pounds, 8 ounces. It was caught by Patricia Simmon in Mormon Lake, Arizona, on July 15, 1989.

Yellow bullhead range.

Yellow bullheads are easy to distinguish from the other major bullhead species in that they have a rounded tail and light-colored chin barbels. The upper barbels are brown.

CATFISH SENSES

The catfish is a marvel of sensory perception, with a set of senses that are unequaled in any other freshwater fish. So acute are the perceptive abilities of this fish that it can hunt, feed and even flourish in total darkness.

SMELL & TASTE

Being river dwellers, catfish are often faced with the challenge of finding food in extremely muddy water. This explains why they are endowed with such an extraordinary sense of smell, which helps them find food even when they cannot see more than a few inches.

Catfish have the most advanced odor-detection system of any freshwater fish.

They have more olfactory folds in their nasal chamber (diagram below) than other fish species, meaning that there are more scent receptors. Channel catfish, for example, have approximately 140 folds, while largemouth bass, smallmouth bass, rainbow trout, crappie and bluegill have only 12 to 24 folds.

Catfish, like sharks, can detect minute traces of amino acids in the water. Blood is particularly rich in amino acids, and the catfish's ability to detect and follow a blood trail is legendary.

While the catfish's sense of smell is useful at a distance, the sense of taste is more important in identifying food items at close range. In most fish, taste buds are found primarily on the lips and in the mouth and throat. But catfish also have taste buds in their barbels and even in their skin. While most fish must actually put food in their mouths to taste it, catfish need only brush it with their barbels or their bodies.

For centuries, anglers have capitalized on the catfish's extraordinary senses of smell and taste. Smelly baits that produce scent trails have long

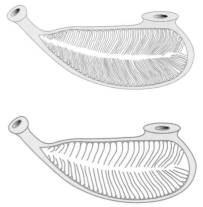

Nasal chamber of catfish (top) vs. largemouth bass (bottom).

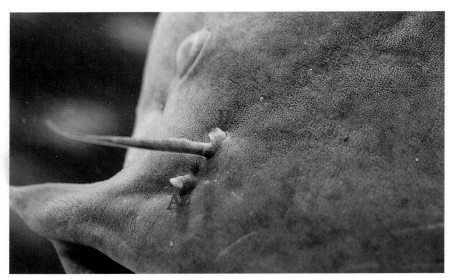
Water enters the nasal chamber through incurrent nares (A) and exits through excurrent nares (B).

been popular, and anglers still pound, mince and slice their cut baits, increasing the amount of amino acids that seep into the water. Astute anglers have also learned the value of "chumming" (baiting) their favorite holes, enticing catfish into the area.

You can also buy dozens of scent products that are poured or sprayed onto lures and baits, supposedly making them irresistible to catfish. Although the actual value of these "potions" is still a topic of debate, some catfish experts swear by them.

SIGHT

The eye of a catfish is quite small when compared to its body size, and tiny when contrasted with the eyes of most other predatory fish. So many anglers mistakenly assume that catfish have poor eyesight, or that they do not use their sense of vision when feeding. In fact, catfish frequently feed on live fish such as shad, carp, drum, bluegill and various min-

nows, and they often rely on eyesight to capture this type of prey.

The vision of a catfish may be less acute than that of a trout, bass, walleye or bluegill, but it is nonetheless a vital sense. In a clear-water environment, vision is probably the catfish's most important sense, especially when it comes to locating live forage.

The eye of the catfish has evolved to complement its night-feeding habits. A structure in the eye, called the tapetum lucidum, functions much like a mirror, reflecting gathered light back over the sensory cells on the retina and improving the fish's dim-light vision.

Most anglers are aware that walleyes have a tapetum, but few realize that the structure is present in catfish. That's because the catfish eye is so small that the glowing tapetum is not nearly as apparent.

A catfish eye has roughly equal numbers of rods and cones. Rods allow black-and-white vision under low-light conditions, while cones allow color vision in daylight.

The tapetum lucidum (glowing area in eye) enables catfish to see well in dim light.

Although there are no major studies of color vision in catfish, indications are that it does exist.

HEARING & THE LATERAL LINE

Catfish detect sound and vibration using two different organs: the ear and the lateral line.

The catfish's ears are located on either side of the head, although there are no openings to pinpoint their location. In water, sound waves are transmitted through the fish's flesh, so external openings are unnecessary.

Like many other animals, catfish detect sounds through their otoliths (ear bones), which vibrate when a sound wave passes through the fish. But catfish have an additional sound-detection mechanism that improves their sense of hearing. When a sound wave passes through the fish and strikes the gas-filled swim bladder, it resonates within the bladder and transfers to the inner ear through a chain of vertebral bones called the Weberian Apparatus.

Intimately tied to the catfish's sense of hearing is the lateral line, a sensory system that detects minute water displacements around the fish. The lateral line is a series of tiny canals with lots of nerve endings that run along the sides of the fish at roughly the midline.

The lateral line detects low-frequency sounds or vibrations that cannot be detected by the fish's ear. Creatures swimming through the water, scuttling across the bottom, plopping onto the surface or stomping along the riverbank ... all create low-frequency vibrations in the water that the lateral line picks up. Catfish use this system to locate prey, identify potential enemies and make it easier for schools to swim in unison.

OTHER SENSES

Some catfish have yet another means of detecting both prey and predators. Tiny pits concentrated on the head and scattered along the body apparently are able to detect minute changes in electrical currents. Apparently, catfish can detect living organisms by simply swimming close to them and monitoring the electrical currents they emit. This can be done in turbid water, in total darkness or even when the prey is buried in sand or mud! This ability has been discovered in many catfish species around the world, but it is not known to what degree large North American catfish utilize this amazing sensory system.

Catfish detect low-frequency sounds or vibrations with their lateral line (arrows).

CATFISHING EQUIPMENT

*T*angling with these whisker-faced brutes requires equipment that is both tough and dependable.

RODS, REELS & LINES

Historically, catfish anglers have used whatever tackle they have on hand. In most parts of the country, that meant bass-fishing gear. While bass tackle is perfectly acceptable for various catfishing chores, experts have discovered that fine-tuning their gear to match a specific catfishing task will usually put more fish in the boat.

The most important consideration when purchasing catfishing tackle is quality. Catfish are as strong as any fish that swim in fresh water, and buying quality tackle is good "insurance" to prevent losing the fish of a lifetime.

CATFISHING RODS

What rod-and-reel combination you select depends on the kind of fishing you'll be doing. Ordinary bass gear will suffice for tossing a gob of nightcrawlers into your favorite stream. Switch to a big live bait, however, and you need a much heavier outfit just to handle your terminal tackle rig.

Similarly, if you normally fish for catfish weighing less than 10 pounds, bass tackle will meet most of your needs. But if you're after a trophy blue or flathead, you must be appropriately armed.

Rod Length

Long fishing rods, those measuring at least 7½ feet, are the best choice for most catfishing tasks. Some anglers swear by rods more than 10 feet long. Here's why long rods work better than short ones:

- A long rod allows you to move more line more quickly, resulting in surer hooksets and increased line control.
- Long rods increase casting distance, which is an especially big advantage for shore fishermen.
- Long rods allow you to "lob-cast" a bait a respectable distance. With a short rod you'll have to sharply snap your wrist to get the same distance, and risk tearing your bait off your hook.
- Long rods give you more "reach" for moving your line in and around cover or controlling your drift in current.
- A long rod, specifically one with a long butt, gives you more leverage for battling trophy cats and helping keep them out of your prop or the brush.

Popular catfishing outfits include a medium-heavy-power spinning outfit (left), flippin' stick with sturdy baitcasting reel (middle) and extra-heavy baitcasting rod and reel (right).

Rod Composition

Most modern catfishing rods are made from fiberglass, graphite or a combination of these materials.

Graphite rods have a much higher "modulus" than fiberglass rods, meaning that they are stiffer for their weight. The higher the modulus, the greater the sensitivity (and higher the price).

A good graphite rod will transmit every quiver of an excited baitfish being eyed by a monster cat, so you know something is about to happen! And even if the bite is extremely subtle, you'll easily be able to feel it.

On the downside, graphite rods are more expensive than fiberglass or composite rods, and considerably less durable. Graphite rods will seldom break when you're fighting a fish, but they are relatively brittle, making them susceptible to quick, sharp bends or blows to the rod tip.

Although fiberglass rods are much less popular than graphite rods, some trophy hunters rely on heavy-duty, fiberglass "pier" rods, used mainly for saltwater angling. Monster cats are not exactly subtle biters, so power and durability are a bigger consideration than sensitivity.

Rods constructed of a fiberglass/graphite composite may be the best all-around choice for catfishing. Look for models with a relatively high percentage of graphite fibers. These rods provide what many catfish experts consider the perfect combination of strength and sensitivity.

CATFISHING REELS

Because the sport traditionally involves heavy line and big fish, the majority of catfish anglers choose baitcasting gear.

A good baitcasting reel should feature:
- Rugged, high-quality construction.
- A free-spool button and a "clicker" that gives you an audible alert when a fish is taking out line.
- A wide spool with plenty of line capacity (at least 150 yards of 20-pound mono).
- A smooth, reliable drag. A sticky drag forces you to keep your drag set too loosely, resulting in weak hooksets and making it impossible to horse fish out of dense cover.

But baitcasting gear is not always the best choice. Whenever you can get by with using light line (12-pound test or less), consider spinning tackle; it works better with smaller-diameter lines and can make a three-pounder feel like a trophy.

Choose a spinning reel with a long, wide spool, which will hold plenty of line and enable longer casts. Be sure the reel has a front drag, which is considerably smoother and more reliable than a rear drag.

A good baitcaster should have a wide spool, a free-spool button and a clicker to signal bites when a fish takes line.

A spinning reel with a long, wide spool casts farther than one with a short, narrow spool. A front drag is smoother and more reliable than a rear drag.

CATFISHING LINES

When you're dealing with fish that routinely exceed the 30-, 40- or even 50-pound mark, it is extremely important that you use top-quality line.

Although premium monofilament lines are still the number-one choice of most catfishermen, "superlines" are making inroads and some catmen swear by braided Dacron.

When selecting mono, abrasion resistance is more important than limpness because you'll often be fishing around logs, pilings, jagged rocks and other cover that could easily scuff your line and weaken it.

Fluorescent mono works extremely well for night fishing because it has a purple glow when exposed to a black light. You can also buy lines that glow bright green or yellow. If you're using several rods at the same time, as many night stalkers do, the bright glow helps you keep track of your lines more easily.

Superlines would seem ideal for catfishing and, in many cases, they are.

Because of their thin diameter, superlines cast well, and the lack of stretch helps you get the solid hook-set necessary to drive a big hook into the jaw of a trophy cat. These lines are also good choices for river fishing because they're less affected by the current.

But superlines have one serious drawback. A sharp edge, such as a broken rock, can easily damage the line and it will part when you attempt to set the hook.

Braided Dacron, though considerably thicker for its strength, is much more abrasion-resistant, making it a better choice in cover that could fray your line.

For all-around catfishing, 17- to 20-pound-test monofilament is a good choice. But if you're a trophy hunter, spool up with a minimum of 25- or 30-pound test. Cats are anything but "line shy," so line diameter is not much of a consideration in catfish angling (except for distance casting). That explains why some trophy specialists use line of 60-pound-test or even heavier.

Regardless of the line they're using, most catfish experts attach a mono leader of anywhere from 20- to 50-pound test. That's because catfish (especially flatheads) have a mouthful of sandpaper-like teeth that can saw through thin line in seconds.

Superline frays easily when dragged across jagged rocks.

Whether you go with monofilament, superline or braided Dacron, toughness is important in catfishing. Shown: (1) Ande Premium, (2) Maxima, (3) Cortland Braided Dacron, (4) Trilene XT, (5) Trilene Big Game and (6) Fusion Spiderwire.

TERMINAL TACKLE

The catfisherman's tackle box is a simple affair, consisting mainly of a variety of hooks, sinkers, swivels and floats.

HOOKS

Your choice of catfish hook depends on the size of the catfish you are likely to catch and the size of your bait.

It's important to carry a wide assortment of hooks. On occasion, you might find a use for hooks in the size 1 to 4 range but, for most catfishing purposes, you'll need size 1/0 to 4/0 hooks. Trophy hunters using giant baits prefer hooks in the 5/0 to 7/0 range.

Any good-quality, standard-length, forged-steel hook will do the job in most catfishing situations. For trotlining, opt for a long-shank hook to make hook removal quick and easy. Many trotliners prefer stainless-steel hooks because they won't corrode. But these hooks are made of softer steel that can bend from the weight of a huge cat and, should your line break, the hook will never rust away.

Some catfish experts think that "keel" hooks (those with an offset bend) dramatically increase hooking success; when a fish bites, the hook automatically turns to penetrate the jaw. Long-shank versions of these hooks work especially well for trotlining because the fish must hook itself.

Circle hooks (the kind used in saltwater fishing) are also gaining in popularity, especially among trotliners or other catfishermen using "absentee" methods. When a fish swims off with the bait, the hook pivots inside the mouth and the fish is almost invariably hooked in the corner of the jaw.

When using a circle hook with a rod and reel, however, do not attempt to set the hook with the normal sharp snap of the wrists. Just let the fish swim off so the line tightens gradually. Then use a smooth, sideways sweep-set to make sure the hook is firmly embedded.

Sharp hooks are important in any type of fishing, but they're especially critical for catfish, which have have thick, tough mouths that can be difficult to penetrate. Be sure to carry a file or whetstone and sharpen your hooks to a needle point. Or, use chemically-sharpened hooks that come with an incredibly sharp point.

Catfish anglers should also carry treble hooks in sizes 4 to 8, for use with congealed-blood and chicken-liver baits. You can also buy trebles with a coiled wire fitted around the shank, for use with dough baits. The wire holds the soft dough firmly on the hook.

SINKERS

It's not unusual to see cat-men and women using rusty bolts, wheel weights, chunks of lead pipe or whatever junk they can find for a sinker. But your success will improve if you carry a variety of sinkers for different bottom types, cover types, depths and current speeds. Another consideration in sinker selection is the buoyancy of your bait.

For most types of catfishing, you'll want to use a slip-sinker rigged so it can slide freely on the line. This way, a cat can swim off with the bait without feeling much resistance, regardless of how much weight you're using. Add a barrel swivel or some other kind of "stop" to keep the sinker from sliding all the way down to the hook.

Egg sinkers are the most widely used catfishing weights, especially in still water. But they tend to roll too much in current, so you're better off with a bell (dipsey) sinker, pyramid sinker or walking sinker (like those commonly used by walleye anglers).

Hooks for catfish include: (1) short-shank, super-strong bait hooks, (2) circle hooks, (3) standard treble hooks, (4) bait-holder treble hook, (5) Aberdeen hooks for catching bait, (6) wide-bend hooks and (7) standard-shank, offset bait hooks.

Hooks, sinkers and swivels comprise the basis of catfishing's terminal tackle arsenal.

Another popular type of catfish sinker is a bottom-bouncer (p. 61). Used mainly for drifting or trolling over a snaggy bottom, a bottom-bouncer enables you to maintain close bottom contact without constant hangups.

For the majority of catfishing situations, use a 1/4- to 1-ounce sinker. In swift water, however, you'll need a sinker weighing from 2 to 6 ounces.

For drifting bait in a stream, pinch just enough split shot on your line to keep the bait slowly bumping along the bottom.

Sinkers for catfishing include (1) split shot, (2) bell sinkers, (3) bank sinkers, (4) pyramid sinker, (5) Rubber Cor sinker, (6) pinch-on sinkers and (7) egg sinkers.

SWIVELS

Besides serving as a slip-sinker stop, a barrel swivel prevents line twist that results from your bait spinning in the current or a catfish rolling when hooked. Without a swivel, you would have to crimp a sinker onto your line and risk damaging it.

Always use high-quality ball-bearing swivels rather than cheap, brass- or tin-plated swivels. A cheap swivel could pull apart, costing you the cat of a lifetime.

When using a slip-sinker rig, it's a good idea to thread a plastic bead onto the line to serve as a cushion between the swivel and the sinker. Otherwise the sinker would butt directly against the knot and possibly weaken it.

Although snap-swivels are seldom used in catfish angling, three-way swivels are necessary for a few specialized rigs.

FLOATS

Versatile catfishermen carry a variety of slip floats for use in keeping the bait at a certain level when catfish are suspended. Floats also work well for keeping your bait drifting naturally along the bottom in current.

The most common style is the "cigar" float, a cylindrical wooden model with a hole down the center. A cigar float is long enough that the top floats high above the waterline, making it easy to see. And it has enough buoyancy to float even a heavy sinker. But any type of slip float, including the inexpensive, oval-shaped styrofoam type, will suffice.

Smaller fixed floats are sometimes added to the leader to float the bait above logs and other obstacles. Most any kind of small clip-on or peg-on float will work for this purpose.

Sharpening Hooks: The Triangular Method

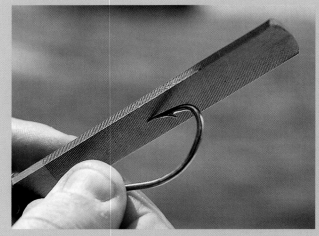

1 File the back side of the point until it has a flat surface.

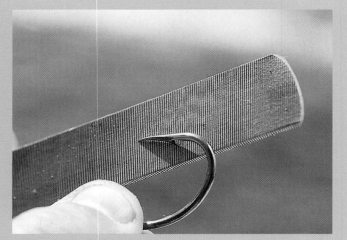

2 Make several strokes with the file on one side of the point.

Popular catfishing floats include: (1) balsa cylinder float, (2) balsa cigar floats, (3) weighted styrofoam float, (4) lighted float with lithium battery, (5) glow-in-the-dark float, (6) styrofoam tube float and (7) peg floats for floating a leader or catching baitfish.

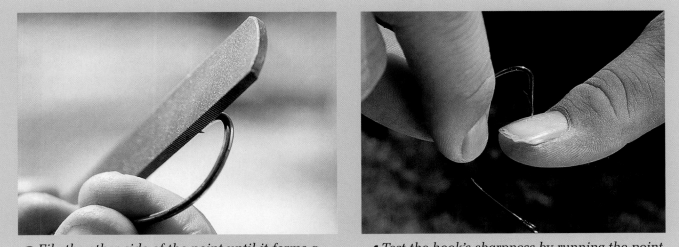

3 *File the other side of the point until it forms a sharp-edged triangle with a very sharp tip. The point's sharp edges and tip help the hook penetrate.*

4 *Test the hook's sharpness by running the point across your thumbnail, as shown. If the point does not catch immediately, the hook is still dull.*

BASIC CATFISH RIGS

Versatile catfishermen know how to tie a variety of rigs for use in both bottom fishing and float fishing. In this section we will show you how to tie the basic rigs, but for some situations you may need variations of these rigs. Those variations will be presented in the "Catfishing Techniques" and "Special Catfishing Situations" sections of this book.

SLIP-SINKER RIGS

Most catfish anglers rely primarily on slip-sinker rigs. In essence, a slip-sinker rig allows the cat to move off with the bait without feeling resistance from the weight, reducing the chances that the fish will drop the bait. Slip-sinker rigs also improve the angler's ability to detect a bite.

The basic slip-sinker rig (tied with an egg sinker) works well in still water or slow current. In faster current, simply replace the egg sinker with a bell, pyramid or walking sinker that will not roll as much.

Most anglers tie their slip-sinker rigs using a barrel swivel as a stop. But some just pinch on a split shot. A swivel holds the sinker more securely so it doesn't slip

down the line, and it allows the angler to use a heavy leader as insurance against line abrasion when fighting a hefty cat.

Some anglers also add a glass or plastic bead between the sinker and the swivel, preventing the heavy sinker from banging against and damaging the knot connecting the swivel to the main line.

In heavy cover, use a slip-sinker rig with a dropper consisting of a piece of monofilament line slightly lighter than the main line, with a pyramid or bell sinker on one end and a barrel swivel on the other. If the sinker becomes snagged, the dropper will break, freeing the rest of the rig.

Some catfish experts thread a small float onto the leader, pegging it in place to float the bait up a little. This places it at eye-level for the catfish and keeps it above most snags.

FIXED-SINKER RIGS

The theory behind a fixed-sinker rig is that catfish are aggressive biters, and they're not going to drop the bait just because they feel a little resistance from the weight. In the majority of cases, this is true, particularly when

you're dealing with big catfish.

There are two basic types of fixed-sinker rigs: those with the hook located in front of the sinker and those with the hook behind it.

Placing the hook in front of the sinker gives you better sensitivity because the fish does not have to move the sinker before you feel the bite.

To make a rig with the hook in front, just tie a double surgeon's loop into the main line, and use a loop-to-loop connection to attach a snelled hook. When fishing for smaller cats, many anglers add a couple of loops and snelled hooks.

Another popular fixed-sinker setup is the 3-way rig. Simply tie a 3-way swivel to your main line, attach a mono dropper with a bell or pyramid sinker to one of the remaining eyes and tie the leader to the third eye. Most anglers use a dropper lighter than the main line; this way, you'll only lose the dropper portion of the rig if the sinker snags.

A 3-way rig, when used with a heavy sinker, works well for bouncing your bait directly under the boat in a river or in the swift-water chutes of a tailrace.

Popular Slip-Sinker Rigs

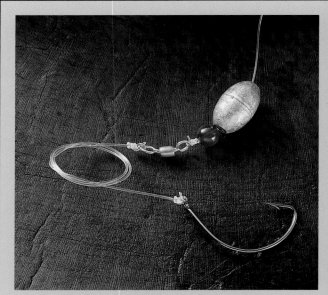

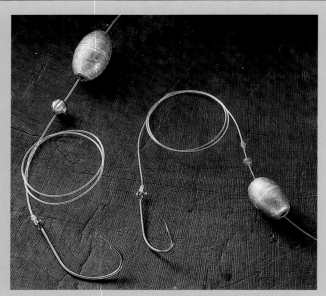

Tie a basic slip-sinker rig by threading an egg sinker and a bead onto your main line, and then tying on a barrel swivel. Finish the rig by tying on a mono leader heavier than the main line and attaching a hook.

Make an adjustable slip-sinker rig for use on a relatively clean bottom by threading on a sinker, adding a split-shot or neoprene stop and then tying on the hook.

Popular Fixed-Sinker Rigs

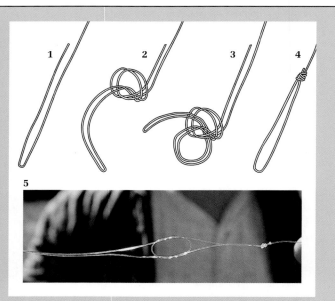

To make a fixed-sinker rig with a front hook, tie a double surgeon's loop in your line (right) and attach a bell or pyramid sinker to the end of your line. Then attach a snelled leader, using a loop-to-loop connection. If desired, make two or three loops and attach leaders to each.

Tie a double-surgeon's loop by (1) doubling the line, (2) tying an overhand knot in it, (3) passing the doubled line through the overhand knot again and (4) pulling on the loop and both lines to snug up the knot. Then, make a (5) loop-to-loop connection by passing the leader loop over the loop you tied and threading the hook through the same loop.

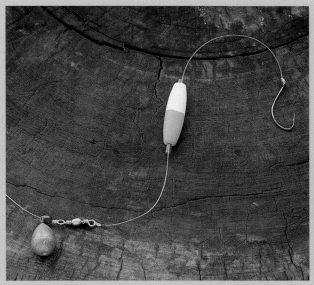

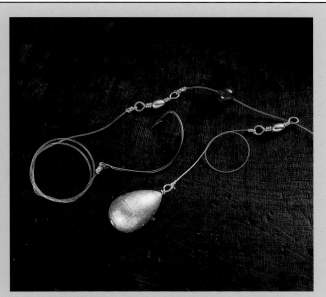

To make a floating rig, thread a crappie float onto your leader and peg it in place with toothpicks. This reduces snagging and keeps the bait at catfish eye level.

Tie a sliding-dropper rig just as you would a standard slip-sinker rig, but substitute a dropper with a bell sinker on one end and a barrel swivel on the other for the egg sinker.

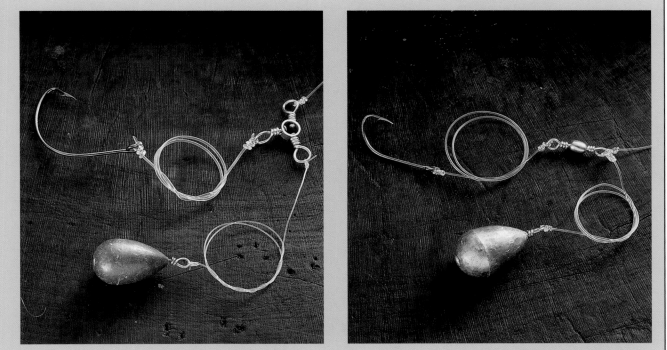

Make a 3-way rig by tying your main line to a 3-way swivel. Attach a dropper with a bell or pyramid sinker to one remaining eye of the swivel and leader and hook to the last remaining eye.

If you don't have a 3-way swivel, you can make a 3-way rig by substituting a barrel swivel. Tie your main line and dropper to one eye and the leader to the other.

FLOAT-FISHING RIGS

Float rigs come in handy for putting your bait in front of suspended cats, and for drifting bait in moving water.

When you're fishing a shallow stream with slow to moderate current, for example, a float often provides a more natural bait presentation. The bait moves naturally downstream, responding to the current, flowing through chutes, skirting around rocks and settling enticingly into pools.

Float-fishing may be the only way to work the eddies that form downstream of boulders, fallen trees and other current breaks. Without a float, the sinker would carry your bait to the bottom and you wouldn't cover the eddy nearly as well.

The type of float rig you use depends mainly on water depth. In water less than 6 feet deep, you can get by with a float that is affixed to your line. In deeper water, however, you'll need a slip-float setup.

Set up a slip-float rig to fish at any depth by simply sliding the "bobber stop" up or down the line. So even if you're fishing in 30 feet of water, you can still reel the bait right up to the rod tip. This way you can easily cast without trying to handle a long length of trailing line.

When the rig hits the water, the sinker pulls the line through the float until it hits the bobber stop.

How much weight you use depends on the size of the float and the current speed. In moving water, it's usually better to pinch on three or four split shot rather than using a single sinker or one large split shot. Crimp the shot onto the line from 4 to 6 inches apart, starting about 12 inches above the hook. This way, the line arcs in the water and the float actually leads the bait downstream, giving you a natural drift and minimizing snags.

For cats suspended in still water, however, a single heavy sinker is a better choice. It will pull your bait down in a hurry and keep it there, even in a strong wind. With a light sinker, the wind will catch your line and drag it through the float, pulling your bait shallower.

A float-fishing rig is perfect for getting at cats hiding in eddies.

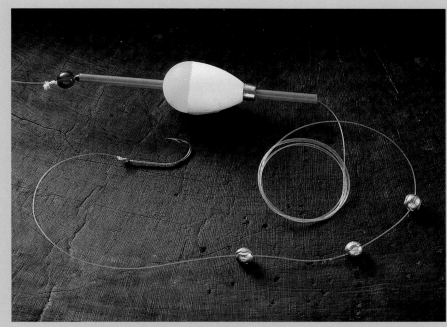

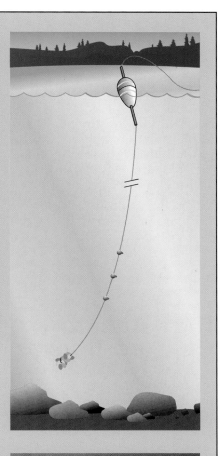

Make a slip-float rig for drift-fishing by tying a bobber stop onto your line and then threading on a bead and a slip float. Tie on a hook and then, starting about a foot up the line, pinch on split shot at 4- to 6-inch intervals until the float is well-balanced. With the shot spread along the line, the float leads the way as the bait skips naturally along the bottom (right).

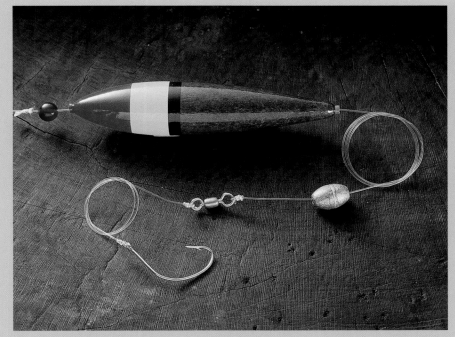

Make a slip-float rig for suspended cats in open water by tying a bobber stop onto your line and then threading on a bead, a slip float and an egg sinker heavy enough to balance the float. Then tie on a barrel swivel and a leader with hook.

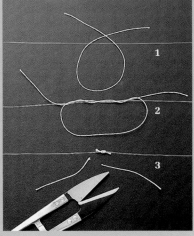

To make a bobber stop, (1) loop a foot-long piece of Dacron line alongside your fishing line, (2) pass the free end of the Dacron line through the loop and around the standing line 4-5 times, (3) pull on both ends of the Dacron line to snug up the knot. Clip long ends.

ACCESSORIES

Anyone who believes that catfishing is a primitive sport that requires only primitive gear hasn't looked in the boat of a modern catfish angler. You'll more than likely see a collection of state-of-the art rods and reels, a quality depth finder and maybe even some sophisticated electronics such as a GPS navigator.

Catfishing also requires an array of special accessories, including the following:

BAIT BUCKET/ CUTTING BOARD

If you've ever tried using the top of your tackle box as a cutting board, you know why savvy cut-bait fishermen often carry a combination bait bucket/cutting board. You can carry baitfish and other natural or prepared baits in the bucket, along with other bait-fishing gear. The top of the container serves as a cutting board, complete with slots for fillet knives and other tools. Unfortunately, these buckets are not on the market so you'll have to make your own (below).

LARGE BAIT BUCKET

An ordinary minnow bucket is of little use in keeping large baitfish alive; it simply doesn't hold enough water. If you're fishing with chubs, suckers or other good-sized baitfish, consider purchasing an insulated, aerated bucket that will keep the water cool and well-oxygenated. It should hold at least 10 gallons of water.

Shad and skipjack herring rank among the top catfish baits, but they're not available in bait shops, so you'll have to catch them yourself (pp. 45-46).

If you plan to use them as cut bait, just toss them into the bait bucket/cutting board described earlier, along with some ice to keep them fresh and moist.

But if you want to keep them alive for longer periods, you'll need a shad tank. Because shad must keep swimming in order to extract enough oxygen from the water, you must use a good-sized tank (20-30 gallons) that is oval-shaped or round. A strong agitator, powered by the boat's 12-volt system, fits on top of the tank and vigorously churns the water to keep it well-oxygenated. A good shad tank

How to Make a Bait Bucket/Cutting Board

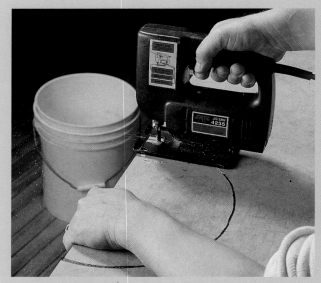

1 Cut a piece of wood to fit across half of the bucket's opening. The wood should fit snugly into the bucket's throat.

2 Drill a few holes through the side of the bucket and screw on the board so it is flush with the bucket's rim. Drill pilot holes and then use a jigsaw to cut knife-holding slits in the wood.

is insulated to keep the water cool, but it doesn't hurt to add some ice on hot days.

Some anglers add commercial shad-care chemicals to the water, but two heaping handfuls of plain rock salt will normally keep the fish in good shape. You may want to add an anti-foaming agent to reduce foam build-up.

To retrieve shad from the tank, use a soft, fine-mesh net from 7 to 8 inches wide, with an 18- to 30-inch handle.

NIGHT LIGHTS

If you plan on fishing after the sun sets, as so many cat-fishermen do, you'll need a gas or battery-powered lantern. Place the lantern well behind you and your rods so you are not blinded by the light.

If you're fishing in a boat, use a lantern holder that clamps to the gunwale or attaches to a rod holder. If the bugs are bad, suspend the light out over the water with a tubular extension.

When night fishing from a boat, a powerful spotlight is a must—not only for navigation, but also for running trotlines, checking limblines and searching for catfishing jugs. Most spotlights connect to a boat's 12-volt system via a lighter socket, although a few are rechargeable. Select one with at least 200,000 candlepower.

Another handy accessory for night fishing is a black light that attaches to your gunwale. These 12-volt ultraviolet lights emit a soft, purple glow that will light up fluorescent mono and make it look like anchor rope for easy line watching.

For tying on and baiting hooks, netting fish or removing hooks from fish, it's hard to beat a battery-powered head-lamp, because it leaves your hands free.

LANDING NET

A large landing net is an important catfishing tool. These powerful fish are slippery, and difficult for novice anglers to land by hand. Without a sturdy net, you could easily lose a trophy fish.

A good catfish net should have a large hoop (at least 24 inches in diameter), a stout yoke and a strong handle that will not bend when you hoist a 50-pounder into the boat. It should also have soft mesh to avoid injuring cats you want to release.

Some cat experts prefer to grab the fish by the lower jaw to prevent injuring it, but a novice shouldn't try this without a heavy leather glove.

FILLET KNIFE

Cut-bait fishermen usually carry several fillet knives and a good sharpener. Sharp knives will save lots of time in filleting the fish and cutting them into bait-sized chunks.

PLIERS

It's a good idea to carry a pair of needlenose pliers for pinching on split shot and straightening hooks, but you'll need a pair of long-handled pliers (such as line-man's pliers) for removing hooks from the maw of a giant cat. If you make the mistake of putting your hand in a big cat's mouth, the tiny recurved teeth could remove a few layers of your skin.

MARKER BUOYS

Markers are useful for pinpointing the location of humps, holes, channel breaks and other drop-offs. Any high-visibility marker will do, but for night fishing you'll need a lighted marker powered by a battery or Cyalume light stick (p. 46). Lighted buoys also work well for marking trotline locations.

ROD HOLDERS

When the term "rod holder" is mentioned, many cat anglers think of the traditional forked stick. But if you've ever watched a big cat swim away with your rod, you know there are better options.

Rod holders designed for bank fishing, for example, consist of a hollow pipe attached to a long stake that is driven into the ground. Because of the angle of pull, a fish cannot jerk the rod out of the holder. On some models, you can even adjust the rod angle.

Boat fishermen use rod holders to increase the number of rods they can effectively handle. Rod holders are a must for drift fishing, and it's not unusual to see boats rigged with six or more sturdy rod holders at strategic locations around the boat.

It's a good idea to buy aluminum or stainless-steel rod holders, either the type that feature a swivel socket at the base or those that fit into mounting bases. With the latter, you can stash the rod holders away when they aren't being used.

Avoid buying cheap, thin-metal, clamp-on rod holders. They will soon begin to rust and probably won't make it through a season of hard use.

How to Throw a Cast Net (Right-Handed Thrower)

In lakes that have them, shad are a top catfish bait. But you can't buy them, so you must catch your own. The best way to do that is by learning to use a cast net.

First, you should know how to select the right net. The differences between a poorly-made cast net and a well-constructed one may not be noticeable, but the difference in performance is quickly apparent. Quality nets cast easier, open flatter, sink quicker and last longer than cheaper versions.

When purchasing a cast net, look for one in which the lead line is double-stitched to the bottom of the net, because much of the strain placed on the net occurs at this point.

Cast nets are measured in feet, according to their radius. A 5-foot net, for example, opens to a diameter of 10 feet. A 5- or 6-foot net is adequate for most anglers, but guides or commercial fishermen who need more bait may use a 7- or 8-footer. As a rule, you'll need at least one pound of lead for every foot of net radius. Of course, larger nets are more difficult to throw.

A monofilament net with $3/8$-inch mesh is ideal for catching shad. A net with smaller mesh sinks too slowly, and larger mesh allows small shad to escape.

1 *Loop the handline around your left wrist, hold coils of the line in your left hand and use the same hand to grasp the rear of the net. Hold the lead line with your right hand.*

2 *Throw the net with your right hand, using your arms and shoulders along with a twisting motion at the waist to spin the net.*

3 *If thrown properly, the net should open into a full circle, land on top of a shad school, and sink quickly to entrap them.*

4 *Let the net sink for a few seconds, then sharply pull on the handline to close the net. Retrieve the net and open it to remove the shad.*

Tips for Collecting Baitfish

Shad are sometimes so thick in tailraces that you can catch them with a dip net. A soft, small-mesh net with a 12-inch hoop and a 7- or 8-foot handle is ideal.

Catch skipjack herring in tailrace areas using an ultralight spinning outfit, 2-pound mono and tiny light-colored flies or jigs. Tie a $^1/_{16}$-ounce jig to the end of your line and attach a series of smaller jigs or flies above it at 8- to 12-inch intervals. You'll often catch several herring at a time.

How to Make a Lighted Marker Buoy

1 Glue a 2- or 3-ounce egg sinker to the cap of a 1-gallon milk jug to make it float neck-down. Attach a cord to the handle and tie on a heavy weight.

2 Crack a Cyalume light stick and insert it so it stands upright in the jug before you set the jug in the water. The light stick will illuminate the entire jug and the glow will last for up to 8 hours.

Other Catfish Accessories

A headlamp is an indispensable night-fishing accessory because it leaves your hands free for rigging and handling fish.

A strong spotlight helps you navigate through stumps and stick-ups and makes it easier to retrieve trotlines, limblines and jugs.

Use a pair of long-handled pliers to unhook deeply-hooked cats. Inserting your hand into a big cat's mouth could result in serious injury.

Wear a heavy glove to hand-land big catfish. Grab the fish by the lower jaw and press on the tongue to keep the fish from closing its mouth.

Mount adjustable rod holders along your boat's gunwales. This way, you can position the rods to cover the maximum amount of water and, at the same time, keep tangling to a minimum.

Push the stake of a bank-style rod holder into the ground until it is firmly implanted. Keep the rod at a sharp angle to the line so a fish can't pull the rod out of the holder.

CATFISHING TECHNIQUES

V *eteran catmen offer sound advice on outwitting channels, blues and flatheads.*

CATFISHING BASICS
TIPS FOR TARGETING CATS

by Don Wirth

The way Jim Moyer approaches catfishing can almost be described as a science. The retired-military-man-turned fishing-guide is widely known for his ability to tar- get different kinds of catfish by working different depth ranges and using fishing methods and baits that specifically appeal to blues, flatheads or channel cats. Amazingly, he can often catch all three from the same boat position.

Moyer's favorite waters are the big rivers near his home in Clarksville, Tennessee, but his techniques can be used anywhere in catfish country.

KNOW THE DIFFERENCE

While the popularity of catfishing has skyrocketed in recent years and catfish are said to be second only to bass in popularity among U.S. anglers, Moyer will tell you that far too many catfish anglers don't know how to consistently locate these fish.

"The main problem most anglers have is that they don't know the differences in the haunts and habits among channel cats, flatheads and blues," Moyer says. "They think all catfish are alike."

"The channel cat's abundance and preference for shallow water have created a great deal of confusion among catfishermen," Moyer explains. "When I first started chasing cats, I fished where everyone else seemed to be fishing—in 10 to 15 feet of water. Naturally, most of the fish I caught were channel cats."

"They were aggressive biters and fun to catch, but I wanted bigger blues and flatheads as well. When I couldn't connect with those fish, I realized I was in the wrong spots. I started exploring different depth zones. That's when I began catching the trophies."

After years of experimentation, Moyer developed a unique targeting system which is based on a solid understanding of the three catfish species.

Channel Cats

Moyer characterizes the channel cat as a roamer. "It's

Channel cats are less dependent on cover than other catfish species.

not a hole-up-and-bite type of fish, but one that prowls wide expanses of water and aggressively hunts for food."

"It tolerates current but doesn't require it. That's one reason this species thrives in ponds and reservoirs. During spring, you can catch channel cats in water as shallow as a foot; most will hold five or six feet deep. And as the water warms to midsummer temperatures, they can still be caught in depths of 10 to 15 feet."

"They like a gravel bottom and a few scattered stumps can't hurt, but they aren't slaves to cover. While flatheads and blues often hunker down in rocks or logs, channel cats are more at home prowling the outside edges of cover."

Flathead Cats

Like channel cats, flatheads are aggressive predators but

spend much of the year in considerably deeper water. Jim's favorite zone for catching these fish is 25 to 35 feet. "I've taken big flatheads down to 55 feet, but only a few. Most are in what I call the mid-depth zone."

Flatheads are known to prefer woody cover—sunken trees, hollow logs, brush piles. "But they also like rock," Moyer adds, "especially sheer bluffs with rubble at the base. I've noticed flatheads have a distinct preference for craggy rock with sharp edges. I think it offers them more places to hide than smooth, round boulders."

Flatheads don't care much for current, preferring slack water or slow-moving eddies instead. And they're perhaps the most nocturnal of all the catfish species, although they will feed in the daytime as well. They usually like a hard bottom, but Moyer has caught some giants from the mud-bottomed lakes of South Carolina's Santee-Cooper reservoir area.

Blue Cats

As for blue catfish, Moyer admits that he was amazed when he began dropping baits into water 35 to 55 feet deep.

"That's when I started connecting with big blue cats, fish I hadn't dreamed existed in the reservoirs and rivers I was fishing." Jim has since caught hundreds of blues that weighed more than 30 pounds from the deep zone.

"This is far deeper than the vast majority of catmen ever fish," he says. "Once, when I brought a 69-pounder back to the ramp so I could weigh it at a local market, an angler came over and demanded to know where I'd caught it. When I told him it came off a 55-foot drop, he didn't believe me and insisted that catfish don't live that deep! For all I know, he's still fishing in shallow water."

"But blues don't like all deep water. They're ledge-oriented creatures," he says. "To hold them, it's got to be a sharp drop, not a slow, gradual descent. They travel up and down the lake or river via these deep channel ledges. They also prefer areas where large objects, especially sunken trees, are scattered along the drop."

Blue catfish will readily eat both live and dead fish, but Moyer prefers cut bait above anything else. "Although they'll take live bait, I use cut bait exclusively because the biggest blues are lazy. They'd rather suck in a big hunk of

Flatheads will not tolerate strong current. They frequently use logs or brush piles as current breaks.

dead meat than exert themselves chasing after a live baitfish."

Forget the tributaries when you're after big blue cats, Moyer suggests. "These are fish of big, deep, open water. You'll find them out in the main channel of a river system or reservoir. Blues thrive in current, much more so than channel cats or flatheads."

Undoubtedly, the most surprising thing Moyer has discovered about blue catfish is how active they are in cold water, as long as there's plenty of current. In fact, he's caught numbers of monster blues when the water temperature barely bumped 36°F!

"Unbelievable as it sounds, these fish actually grow more aggressive the colder the water gets, as long as there's good current flow. But when the hydroelectric dam stops generating power (meaning the gates have been closed), the fish shut off almost instantly."

SHALLOW-WATER METHODS

Fishing shallow-water cats is fun and requires little in the way of specialized gear, Moyer says. "When channel cats and flatheads are shallow, especially in the spring, I fish a gob of nightcrawlers or a lively minnow under a float. I'll pitch the bait close to the cover, then reel the float slowly back to the boat. A stiff spinning rod and 10-pound line are perfect for the cats you'll typically encounter here."

Float rigs are especially handy for bank fishermen, Moyer adds. The rigs keep the bait suspended and help prevent annoying hangups.

DEEP-WATER METHODS

Fishing deeper requires an anchor and a dependable depth finder. "Wind and current can make it very difficult or impossible to stay on a spot that's much more than 20 feet deep," Moyer emphasizes. "I use a 35-pound anchor because I target giant blue cats in swift river current, but you can get by with a lighter one where there's less current."

When probing a deep river ledge, Moyer starts in deep water and then slowly motors toward the bank, watching his sonar screen. "If the bottom rises slowly and steadily, I keep moving, but when it jumps up quickly, I circle back around and drop anchor on the high side of the ledge. I let out just enough anchor line to keep the boat from slipping downstream. The anchor is attached to the bow; we fish out of the stern."

Blue cats are the most current-oriented catfish species.

Moyer next prepares his bait. "Big blues and flatheads love cut bait fished right on the bottom. I use fresh-caught skipjack herring, a firm but oily fish commonly found below dams across the South. They have plenty of odor and taste appeal and work far better than prepared stinkbaits."

Moyer scales the large baitfish, then fillets and cuts it into chunks. The chunks are stacked on a stout hook at the business end of a slip-sinker rig. The baited hooks are then staggered along deep ledges.

"I put my inside line (the one closest to shore) in the 30- to 35-foot zone, well away from the drop-off. This is the bait that'll most often attract a big flathead. The middle line is placed as close to the drop as I can get it, again around 35 feet. This one will pick up big flatheads or blues that are cruising the ledge. The outside line is positioned at the bottom of the drop, sometimes as deep as 55 feet. This is the one that the giant blue cats will most often hit."

A lack of heavy current flow is the one factor that will cause Moyer to alter his game plan. "If the flow is very light, I put my deepest line in the 35-foot zone and fan the other two out at the 25-foot depth. These baits target flatheads, which are more active in the slack water."

Moyer looks for more than drop-offs on his depth finder. He also watches for scattered cover and baitfish as well. "I don't like to fish in dense cover because you constantly get hung up. Or, you lose a lot of big fish that run into trees and rocks once they are hooked. Instead, I look for scattered, isolated objects, especially a sunken tree or big rock, along the drop. But the key to these types of spots is the presence of baitfish. If they aren't there, the going gets tough. Big catfish are eating machines, and they need to be around a consistent food supply."

TESTING THE SYSTEM

I recently joined Moyer for an on-the-water demonstration of his catfish-targeting method. We were more interested in catching big flatheads and blues than channels, so Moyer anchored his boat on a deep river ledge. He then cast one line to the wide shelf on top of the ledge in 30 feet of water. The middle line was positioned close to the drop-off at 35 feet, while the outside line was at the bottom of the drop—55 feet deep.

After "warming up" on a small blue that hit the shal-

When fishing a deep ledge, the top line (1) is most likely to catch flatheads; the middle line (2), flatheads and blues; the bottom line (3), giant blues.

low line and slugging it out with a beautiful 24-pounder on the middle line, the action ground to a halt.

"Just like somebody turned off a switch," I commented after 30 minutes of staring at the motionless rod tips. "Maybe we'd better try another spot."

"Sometimes when the small cats suddenly quit biting it means a big one has moved in," Moyer said matter-of-factly. Then as if on cue, the tip of the outside rod started to dip. It continued bending toward the water, until I grabbed it and set the hook.

The monster cat loaded up the heavy-duty stick, and even though the level-wind reel's drag was set tight, the fish ripped off line in short, angry bursts. It was so strong I began to wish I was strapped into a fighting chair.

Fifteen minutes went by, then 20. The rod was beginning to feel like a telephone pole, and the cat like an Oldsmobile stuck in low gear. Finally, it moved off the bottom and I was able to use what was left of my strength to crank it to the boat. The blue cat weighed nearly 60 pounds.

I'll never forget that day, for it introduced me to an entirely new catfishing system. And the more I fish for these great gamefish, the more I realize how important it is to understand the unique qualities of each species.

Author Don Wirth and his trophy blue.

Moyer's Targeting Tips

	CHANNEL CATS	FLATHEAD CATS	BLUE CATS
CURRENT SPEED	Slow	Slight to none	Moderate
IMPORTANT COVER/STRUCTURE	Patrols outside edges of stumps, rocks, logs	Sunken trees, hollow logs, brush piles, rocks	Sharp ledges, scattered sunken trees
PROXIMITY TO COVER	Tends to roam	Linked tightly to cover	Loosely associated
NORMAL DEPTH RANGE	10-15 feet	25-35 feet	35-55 feet
PRIME FEEDING TIME	Moderately nocturnal	Strongly nocturnal	Moderately nocturnal
MOST EFFECTIVE BAITS	Live bait, cut bait, prepared bait	Live baitfish, cut bait	Cut bait

HOT TIME FOR COOL CATS

by Keith Sutton

Joe Drose on his party barge.

Catfish guide Joe Drose sits smiling behind the wheel of his huge party barge, keeping a close watch on the four rods in holders that are bolted onto the bow railing. A cold February breeze is blowing across South Carolina's expansive Lake Marion, but the pontoon's transparent cabin cover stops it short.

Marion and her sister, Lake Moultrie, are the gems of the Santee-Cooper area, a system of lakes and rivers famous for their outstanding bass, crappie and catfish fishing. Drose knows the water better than most.

Along with my fishing companions Lewis Peeler and Mark Davis, I'm enjoying the warmth of the boat's cabin as Drose shares the wisdom he has gained after nearly 40 years of fishing these waters.

"Catfish aren't like us," Drose says. "They don't care how cold it is, they will eat. Some fisherman still refuse to believe how good fishing can be during the dead of winter, but it's not unusual to catch several 20-pound-plus cats a day—even when the air temperature is freezing. In fact, a number of my biggest fish have come in December, January and February."

"Striper fishing used to draw folks here from all around the country," he says. "There weren't any flathead or blue cats in the lakes at all. Then in 1964, the state's fisheries department started trading South Carolina stripers for Arkansas blue cats."

"The blues did so well, they began stocking flatheads, too. Eventually, the striper fishing tapered off, and in the mid-1980s, catfishing boomed."

"Soon, anglers started catching giant cats—fish weighing more than 50 pounds—on a fairly regular basis, and it hasn't let up a bit. Today your chances of catching trophy-class blues or flatheads up to 70 or 80 pounds are outstanding. And there are loads of channel cats up to 15 or 20 pounds, too. Nowadays I guide only anglers who

want catfish, and it keeps me on the water nearly every day of the year."

On a previous trip, Mark's wife, Kathy, landed a 69-pound blue, a 24-pound flathead and an 18-pound channel cat while fishing with Drose. Mark didn't do quite as well. His biggest fish that trip was "only" a 50-pound blue.

So far, our luck hasn't been as good. We've landed two 5-pound-plus channel cats, but the monsters refuse to bite. Joe blames their lack of activity on a low-pressure system that is moving through the area.

Suddenly, one of the rods takes a nosedive. Lewis is beside it and makes the hookset. Something hefty surges away, stripping 30-pound mono off the reel. "Feels like a good one," he says, "but not a monster."

The fish puts on an impressive show, but Lewis soon swings it over the transom. It's another nice channel cat weighing about 8 pounds. "Where's your grandpappy?" Lewis asks, twisting the hook from the fish's lip.

What surprises me most is how icy-cold these fish are. Each fights like the dickens, yet when we touch one fresh out of the water, it feels like a popsicle. How, I wonder, can these cold-blooded creatures put up such a fight when their body

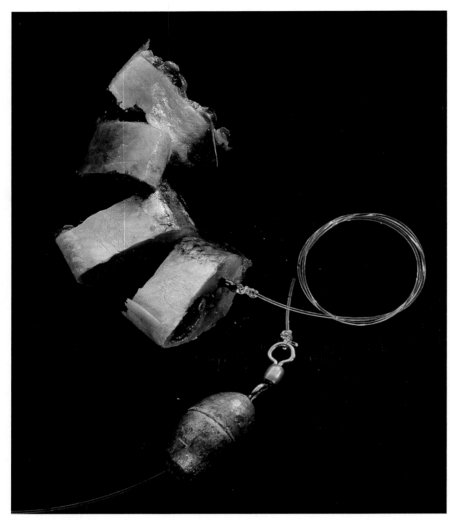

Thread a 1-ounce egg sinker onto your line and then add a barrel swivel, a 12-inch leader and a size 3/0 to 5/0 Kahle hook baited with cut shad or herring.

Keeping your hook point exposed will improve hooking—and landing—ratios.

temperatures are barely above freezing?

GEARING UP

Because winter catfish often gather in small areas to feed at this time of year, Drose usually anchors his boat and still-fishes using sturdy tackle—7-foot Shakespeare Ugly Stick Tiger Rods and Shakespeare bait-casting reels spooled with 25- to 80-pound test monofilament line. Drose uses the heavier line when fishing areas with lots of stumps and other cover, to reduce the chance of a big cat breaking off.

For most of his winter fishing, Drose relies on a simple egg-sinker rig baited with fresh-cut shad or herring (opposite).

"I sometimes use commercial dip bait like JoJo's Supreme Sewer Bait or pieces of hot dogs, too," he says. "These are about the same size as the small mussels the catfish are feeding on, and they seem to work real well."

"A lot of times if a piece of bait is too large, a catfish will swim right by it and go for a smaller bait instead. So it's important to use bait that is not too big, even when you're fishing for trophy-class fish."

"Most of the time we use small herring for bait," he continues. "Although the catfish are feeding primarily on mussels, they won't pass up a piece of herring that's properly presented. I cut each herring into small chunks, and use the entire fish. But for some reason, the head always seems to draw more strikes."

"Run the hook through the belly part of the fish, because

Catfishing Strategies

that's where it's the thinnest, and leave the hook exposed. If you cover your whole hook with bait, when a fish bites you don't have anything left to hook him with."

Joe uses laser-sharpened Kahle hooks because they hook clean and hold fish.

SHALLOW-WATER METHODS

In winter, Drose focuses most of his efforts in shallow water, fishing broad flats on the edges of creek channels. Most of the time he fishes in just 2 to 6 feet of water, far shallower than I expected to find winter fish.

Once he's on the water, Drose becomes a hunter, searching for big cats feeding in the shallows. He won't stay in one location longer than 20 minutes or so unless he's into fish.

In fact, Drose thinks winter catfishing is almost like bass fishing. The angler doesn't just sit in one spot waiting for something to happen. He keeps on the move, trying one area, then another. Some stretches of bank won't yield a single fish, but others may produce a big catfish on every cast.

"The vast majority of the catfish we catch in winter are blues and channels," Drose notes. "Flatheads don't start biting good until the water warms up in May. Blues and channels, however, are active feeders year-round. I've caught them when it was so bone-cold out here that you could barely turn the reel handle when you hooked a fish."

"Most winters, blues move to sand edges in shallow water and stuff themselves on small mussels."

"When the lake level is down, I search for the mussel beds, then come back and fish them after the water rises again because that's where the biggest and most cats are likely to be."

"Generally the rougher the water is, the better the fishing is in shallow water, if you can keep your boat properly anchored," he notes. "I do all my fishing throughout the year during daylight hours. When there's a sharp breeze, it's stirring up the bottom in the shallows, moving food around. The catfish don't pay as much attention to the boat then as they do when it's calm, either."

"I also seem to do best on clear, sunny days," he adds. "The fish move around more then, and you get a lot more action. When it's cloudy, they'll get somewhere and just sit; they don't seem to move around a lot. You have to drop a bait right in front of one to get a bite."

DEEP-WATER METHODS

There are times, of course, when channel and blue catfish leave the shallow mussel beds to feed on other forage. This is especially true during extended periods of severe cold that cause

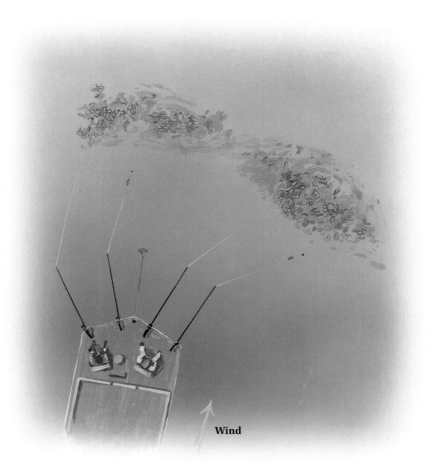

Wind

Mussels lie in dense beds in shallow water, drawing hungry winter cats. Use a double anchoring system (one off the bow and one off the stern) to hold the boat securely in one location, and make long casts to the fish. Space lines as far apart as possible to cover water.

When an extended cold snap drives water temperatures down below 45°F, threadfin shad become distressed and die in large numbers. Being opportunistic feeders, catfish often stack up beneath baitfish schools and gorge themselves. To take advantage of this situation, use sonar to locate a school of shad, then drop your baits to about a foot from bottom to prevent snagging. A single dead shad hooked through the eyes is a tough bait to beat in this situation.

threadfin shad die-offs. When the water temperature first dips below 45°F, usually in December or January, cold-stressed shad attract enormous concentrations of hungry catfish.

"As the shad start dying and filtering toward the bottom, catfish by the hundreds move under those big schools of baitfish," Drose maintains. "They gorge on the crippled shad as they drift down. This pattern may last three to four weeks at a time."

When this is happening, search for the shad with your sonar. When you locate a school, use a cast net to collect bait. The smaller shad—those just an inch or two long—seem to work best. Hook two or three at a time on a single hook, running the hook through the eyes and leaving the barb exposed. Then lower your rig to the bottom, reel it up

about a foot, and get ready for the action that's likely to follow.

When the catfish are really gorging on shad, you can't fish more than one rod per angler because they're biting so fast. You may drop a bait down, reel it up a bit, and before you set the rod in the holder you'll have a big one on. Then you remember why you're out there fishing on such a cold day.

Before our day of winter catfishing was over, I had photographed Lewis and Mark grinning with 51- and 39-pound blue cats they had wrestled onto Drose's party barge. Each was popsicle-cold to the touch, just like the many

jumbo channel cats we also caught that day.

If you're like most catfishermen, you put your rods away when the water gets cold, but as Joe Drose has proven, that's a big mistake. Give his methods a try on your waters—you could be in for a giant surprise.

A good sonar unit is important for locating fish, structure and bait. These cats are holding on the edge of a fairly deep channel. In this situation, they are likely to be feeding on temperature-stressed shad filtering down from schools holding near the surface.

Mark Davis with his 39-pounder.

The Drift-Fishing Option

Though Drose generally fishes from an anchored boat, he will drift fish when dealing with widely scattered cats. In winter, catfish are usually concentrated in loose schools in small areas. For this reason, most anglers anchor their craft and fish each area thoroughly. When this tactic proves ineffective, however, drift fishing may save the day.

Drose uses a float rig when drifting. He runs the main line through the eye of a bottom bouncer or pencil weight, with a barrel swivel below it to keep the weight from sliding down. A 12- to 18-inch leader is then tied to the other eye of the swivel, with a small float affixed to the middle of the leader. A 3/0 Kahle hook finishes off the end. The float suspends the baited hook above the bottom to help prevent snags.

To slow his drift on windy days, Drose employs two custom-made sea anchors, each six feet in diameter, which he attaches to his party barge with short lengths of nylon rope. The wind pushes the craft along while the anchors slow the drift.

Drose watches his depth finder while drifting, using his outboard to follow creek channels and other structure where catfish are likely to hold.

Drose's bottom-bouncer rig.

PROSPECTING FOR BLUES

Generations of catmen have heeded the doctrine, "If you fish the right spot long enough, they will come."

And they often do.

It's hard to dispute the fact that still-fishing is one of the deadliest catfishing methods. But some of the country's top catmen would certainly try.

Neither anchors nor rod holders figure into the fishing equation, for instance, when Glen Stubblefield targets catfish. A master catfish guide on Kentucky Lake, he opts for the active approach, assigning one rod per angler (always in hand) and continuously running his trolling motor.

With patient persistence, Stubblefield picks his way along stump-laden ridges washed by strong main-lake currents, plucking fish from the murky breaklines beneath the hull of his boat.

Keith McCoy and Joe Rodgers don't hang around waiting for cats to come to them, either. Tournament-champion catmen from Fremont, Nebraska, McCoy and Rodgers prospect for catfish by drifting across vast, open waters, bouncing blood baits along the bottom.

As McCoy proudly proclaims, "We go after them."

The two enterprising Nebraskans stunned the catfish establishment on South Carolina's Santee-Cooper one fall when they used their drift-fishing tactics to win the National Championship Catfish Tournament. They boated 235.5 pounds of catfish, including a hefty blue

McCoy and Rodgers with their 70.5-pounder.

that weighed 70.5 pounds and took big-fish honors in the tournament.

Although the Stubblefield method differs somewhat from the McCoy/Rodgers method, both are equally effective.

STUBBLEFIELD'S METHOD

Glen Stubblefield's favorite strategy allows him to thoroughly work a piece of prime structure. It also keeps the minnows he favors as bait just off the bottom, where catfish are most apt to find them.

It's a demanding task. Heavy currents in the areas he fishes call for constant attention to the trolling motor and depth finder, while ever-changing bottom contours demand that lines be continually raised and lowered.

Stubblefield earns his living on Kentucky Lake, an expanse of water that stretches over 184 miles and covers more than 163,000 surface acres in Tennessee and Kentucky.

He quickly narrows his search, however, by fishing only the lower third of the lake, sticking to the main Tennessee River portion. He looks for the ideal combination of bottom structure, cover and current.

"You see a lot of water out here," he says, his arm tracing an imaginary arc both up- and downstream. "But you won't see me fish very much of it."

Major bends in the old river channel, points that stretch out toward a channel drop, and noteworthy humps rising from an otherwise flat bottom provide the kind of structure that Stubblefield seeks. Prime cover comes in the form of stump fields or flooded homesteads.

Glen Stubblefield hoists in an impressive blue.

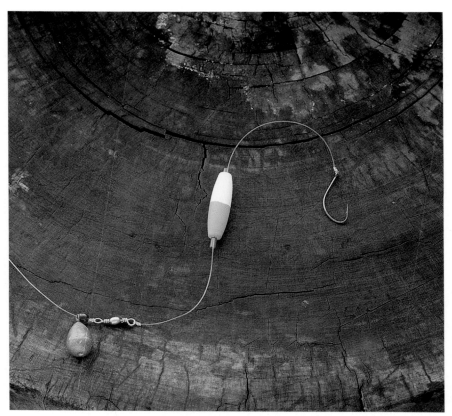

Stubblefield's tight-line rig consists of a 3-way swivel spliced into the line about a foot above a 1-ounce bell sinker, and a 6-inch dropper with a size 1 hook.

Current flows in the main lake whenever water is being run through the dams, creating another key element in Stubblefield's catfish system—moving water.

During periods of slack water, Stubblefield is forced to work the upstream side of islands, narrow cuts and inside various necked-down areas where there is still some current.

"The catfish are much more active in flowing water—and the stronger the current the better," he explains. "Sometimes when they turn on the water at one of the dams, it's just like flipping a switch. The catfish start feeding like crazy."

Stubblefield's active approach allows him to work his way through areas that offer a combination of fish-attracting features. Contrast this to the stationary catman, who must be satisfied with

Push the hook through the eye of baitfish and out the side to create a bend, as shown. This gives the bait considerably more action in current.

the attributes of only one spot—often a happy medium of cover and current, but seldom the best combination all day, every day.

For example, a creek's confluence with the Tennessee River channel near a stump-studded bend in the channel would be great, but such an area would be even better if there was a hole from an old pond nearby. Add a major island downstream to split and strengthen the river's flow and you're in cat heaven. By slow-trolling, Stubblefield can cover all of these important bases.

He uses a tight-line rig with a 1-ounce bell sinker at the end and a size 1 hook tied to a 6-inch dropper a foot or so above the weight. A fresh minnow is threaded onto the hook through the eye and out the

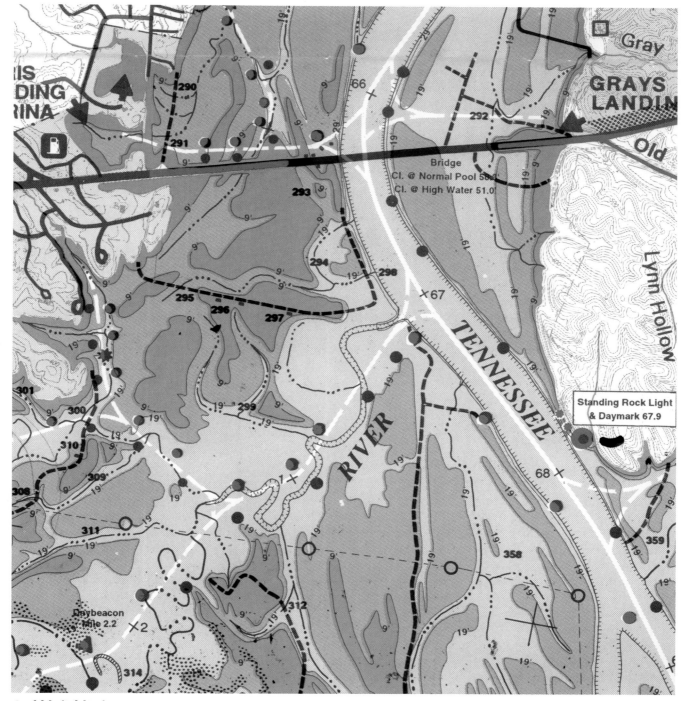

Stubblefield's favorite strategy is to stay on the move to actively find cats in their haunts.

Catfish have an uncanny ability to detect blood and body fluids oozing from the bait.

side (p. 64), so that its body is bent slightly by the curve of the hook. This usually kills the minnow but the angle of its body causes the dead bait to flutter in the current.

The line is kept tight, with the weight touching bottom but not dragging across it. "You should barely bump the bottom with the bell sinker," Stubblefield advises. "Otherwise, snags eat up more lines than catfish."

With each angler holding a rod, reeling in or releasing line as needed, Stubblefield uses the trolling motor to slowly crawl upcurrent. Often he follows the edge of a drop or trolls across a stump-laden hump, never taking his eye off the depth finder as he follows each crease and wrinkle.

While he normally works an area very thoroughly—especially if the cats are cooperative—Stubblefield won't stay long in an area if the fish aren't biting. There are just too many other good spots on Kentucky Lake to waste time waiting for a particular bunch of catfish to turn on.

Newcomers to Stubblefield's style of fishing tend to hook a lot of stumps. It's understandable—with the boat moving, current flowing and adrenaline pumping, the stumps do feel a lot like strikes—and the hook usually gets set pretty hard.

Veteran tight-liners, however, recognize the stumps for what they are and finesse the bait over the tops, then prepare for a strike. For some reason, the rig sliding off the upcurrent side of a stump often triggers a hit.

The relationship between cats and wood is so strong that even when one of his clients gets snagged, Stubblefield looks for a strike on another line. He's not often disappointed.

Strikes, especially from big fish, typically feel like nothing more than extra weight on the line—only a subtle difference in the apparent weight of the rig separates fish from snag.

For example, Stubblefield had just bumped his sinker against a stump last summer when his rod tip began to dip. "Big fish never hit the bait hard," he muses, "they just start moving off, pulling the rod down slowly as they go." True to form, that stump-hugging blue weighed close to 50 pounds.

Blues comprise the bulk of Stubblefield's catch, with channel cats next in line and flatheads showing up only on occasion. He surmises that the reason bumping the stumps works better for channels and blues is because both species typically jump on a bait pretty fast if it looks and smells appealing. A moody flathead, on the other hand, will often stare at a bait before deciding to grab it.

Stubblefield has caught blues weighing up to 65 pounds, but fish ranging in size from 5 to 15 pounds are his bread and butter. Even these "smaller" cats put up a tremendous battle on his standard tight-line outfit, an Ambassadeur 5500 reel strung with 20-pound test and a medium-action rod.

Tight-line catfishing requires well-defined structural features—as well as steady current—to hold the bait off bottom and make the fish more aggressive.

Although Stubblefield concentrates on the impounded waters of Kentucky Lake, his method also works on big rivers. Use your electronics to slowly work the channel edge, drop-offs and other well-defined, cat-holding breaklines.

McCoy & Rodgers' Method

McCoy and Rodgers spread their lines over whatever type of bottom happens to be beneath their boat—as long as they're marking catfish and bait on their electronics—and let the wind dictate the direction of their drift.

The Nebraskans aren't so "civilized" when it comes to bait—they rely on stomach-turning cubes of coagulated cow blood to entice big cats.

"The blood is both a bait and an attractant," McCoy explains. "We bring the bait to the catfish, but as we drift along, the blood also leaves a scent trail. Any fish that crosses this trail can follow it right to our baits."

After the proper aging, the blood forms a coagulated, gelatin-like mass that is easily threaded onto a leader and held in place on a treble hook. As the bait drifts along, the blood slowly dissolves in the water, leaving a path of scent particles that hungry cats can't pass up.

The process actually begins with all lines still in the boat, especially on unfamiliar waters. McCoy uses his depth finder to study the lake bottom. He looks for catfish and baitfish scattered over large flats or holding on sunken islands and other structure, and marks the depths at which each is holding.

McCoy also searches for areas where shallow and deep water are close to one another, offering catfish easy access to various depths. Such a situation also gives the men the opportunity to place baits in a range of depths in a single drift.

Although finding the right depth is critical, McCoy notes, there is no magic depth for every drift. That can change from day to day, and lake to lake.

"It may take a couple of hours to find the fish some days," he says. "But once you discover the right depth for the bigger cats, you can figure on finding more at the same level."

If McCoy catches small catfish, or marks them with his sonar, he shifts to different depths, having learned from experience that little catfish typically give the big boys a wide berth.

When McCoy and Rodgers find what looks like a potentially productive section of water, they motor well upwind and then set their lines for a drift. Dragging one or more sea anchors to control boat speed and direction, they drop their baits to the bottom and begin a slow pass that will commonly last about an hour.

Often they begin a drift over open water, pass over the structure and keep drifting all the way into shore. When the boat comes to rest, they leave their lines in the water for another 10 minutes or so before reeling in to try the process again.

While trolling slowly upstream, lower your rig deep enough that the sinker, but not the bait, barely bumps stumps, rocks and other bottom debris.

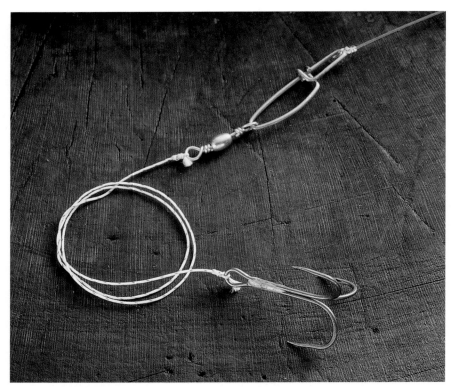

The basic blood-bait rig consists of a foot-long, 100-pound test Dacron leader with a size 1 to 2/0 treble hook on one end and a barrel swivel on the other.

"Sometimes catfish will follow the blood for a long time, but they won't take it until it stops and settles onto the bottom," McCoy explains.

The blood bait is strung onto a leader—a foot-long section of 100-pound braided Dacron that is not yet attached to the main line. To get the blood onto the leader, McCoy and Rodgers use a 6-inch piece of thin, stiff wire. When pressed against the barrel swivel at the top of the leader, the wire acts like a needle, helping thread the blood onto the line.

The chunk of blood bait slips down the leader onto a treble hook (size 1 to 2/0, depending on the size of the bait). The leader is then attached to a snap tied on the end of the main line and the bait is dipped in the water for a few minutes to toughen it before dropping it to the bottom.

McCoy and Rodgers seldom use sinkers with their blood bait. Except in heavy wind, current or deep water, the blood is heavy enough to stay on the bottom without additional weight.

Their terminal tackle varies little wherever they fish, but the rods, reels and main line they use may change from lake to lake, depending on the size of the catfish they expect to encounter.

Channel catfish up to 20 pounds dominate the fisheries in the lakes McCoy and Rodgers typically target around home, and they proved at Santee-Cooper that drifting blood also works great for trophy-size blues.

The tactic is less effective for flatheads, which prefer live bait.

Drifting works well on unfamiliar waters. That's a plus for the pair because it allows them to cover a lot of territory when looking for catfish.

McCoy says that no matter where they roam, they always start with the same basic system, then let current conditions dictate the specifics.

"You have to pay attention to wind strength and direction, water depth, bottom structure, baitfish, the mood of the cats—and make adjustments as you go," he says.

Once the blood is on the hook, attach the leader to a clip on your main line. Unless there is a strong wind or current, no sinker is necessary.

Catfishing Strategies

How to Make and Fish Blood Bait

Over the years, McCoy and Rodgers have perfected a unique method for preparing coagulated blood as fishing bait.

They obtain cow blood from a local slaughterhouse and cool it in a bucket for five days at 32°F until it forms an unappetizing mass with about the same consistency as gelatin. The blood is then poured onto a hard, level surface, flattened into a pancake shape about an inch thick, allowed to congeal, and then cut into squares that vary in size from about 1 to 3 inches across.

"We typically use smaller pieces of blood bait early in the season, when the fish are a little more tentative," says McCoy.

1 *Pour the coagulated blood onto a flat, non-porous surface, roll it into an inch-thick mass and allow it to congeal.*

2 *Cut the coagulated blood into 1- to 3-inch squares. Store the bait in resealable plastic bags.*

3 *Use a stiff wire as a needle, holding it next to the barrel swivel and pushing the swivel and leader through the blood bait.*

4 *Slide the blood bait down the leader and impale it on the treble hook.*

SPRING FLING FOR CATS

By Dan Gapen

High water rolled and boiled from beneath the gates of Pickwick Dam on the Tennessee River. The spring run of sauger had all but ended, though a few die-hards were still banging heavy rigs along the bottom as they drifted downstream. Most locals had turned to their favorite sport—the pursuit of Tennessee River catfish. It was late March.

Pulling up to the boat ramp below the huge dam, my buddy, "Bobber Anne," posed the question. "Dan, what do you think?"

"Dunno Anne, but the weather's nice and reports I received from Hank say the cats are on."

Hank Perkins, a local bait dealer, had responded posi-

The spring catfish run draws hordes of anglers to popular tailrace areas.

tively to my inquiry about catfishing when I called him two days previously. Hank knows when conditions are right on the Tennessee.

With boat launched and gear stowed, we set out, our destination the twin metal pilings a quarter mile downstream from the dam face. We pulled up below the pilings and killed the motor. Our anchor grabbed hold a few seconds later.

Anne baited up with chicken liver; I chose cut shad. We cast directly downstream from our anchored boat, some 100 feet below the last metal piling. As the morning sun began to warm both anglers and surroundings, our wait began.

THOSE DAM CATS

All over North America, river dams draw catmen. Big rivers such as the Mississippi, Tennessee, Ohio, Missouri, Hudson and Alabama all have dams that prevent the upstream migration of many gamefish species, catfish included.

Tailwater areas also hold a plentiful supply of cats on small rivers such as the Oncee in Georgia, Vermillion in Kansas, Red in North Dakota and Manitoba, Fox in Illinois, Buffalo in Iowa, Snake in Minnesota and Castor in Missouri.

Tailwaters are ideal feeding grounds for cats in the spring. There are immense gravel and rock flats, deep holes, and all have a constant flow of water.

There's also plenty of food. The dam's turbines or massive

Imagine battling a cat like this after a long winter off the water.

floodgates funnel shad, rough fish and other critters through the dam to become easy pickings for the catfish waiting below. Often the only problem an angler has during spring's high-water periods is that there is too much food available.

Food availability is the reason all species of catfish remain below dams long into the season, even after other gamefish have retreated downstream to their summer feeding grounds.

All dams, big or small, have holes a short distance downstream called "washouts" or "digouts." These holes are created by

water rushing through the dam and are usually occupied by catfish waiting for settling food.

Channel cats begin moving up to the dams in early spring when the water temperature nears the 60°F mark. Fishing in washout holes can be incredible during the pre-spawn period.

Numbers of smaller cats, mainly channels, can often be plucked from humps directly downstream from the washouts, in shallow water with moderate current. You can take fish off both the up- and downstream sides of these humps.

The best humps are usually within 500 feet of the dam. They're created by fast water dislodging gravel, rock and sand below the dam apron and then depositing it downstream from the washout. Humps vary in size. Some are large and high, others are small, but practically every tailrace has them.

During the spring, all species of cats tend to feed throughout daylight hours, which makes for enjoyable daytime angling.

That March morning, it took just four minutes for the first fish of the day to inhale Anne's chicken liver and take

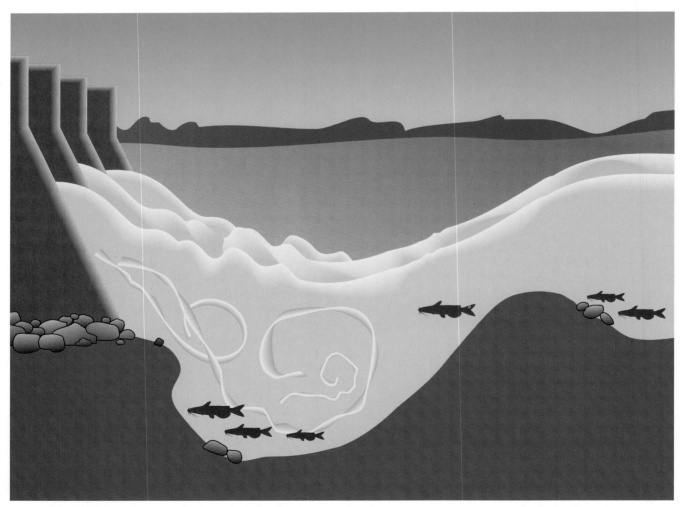

A washout hole makes an ideal catfish feeding area. The fast current passes over the hole, forming an eddy where catfish can get out of the current and grab any food items that settle out. Cats also congregate on humps downstream from washouts.

off cross-current. There was no "tap-tap" so familiar to summer catfish anglers, just the hit-and-run bite of a cold-water cat.

Anne's catfish fought well. Several minutes passed before she could lift it over the boat gunwale. Scale weight registered at 8½ pounds, a decent channel cat and a nice start!

A few minutes later I had a hard rap, then it was off to the races once again. This fish, at 10 pounds, fought even harder than Anne's; and instead of a channel catfish, it turned out to be a blue.

Within a couple of hours, Anne and I had caught 18 channel cats, three blues and one flathead, releasing them all. Not bad, considering three of the fish weighed better than 20 pounds.

GEARING UP

Nightcrawlers, fresh cut shad and frozen chicken livers produce best for channel cats during the spring months, when water temperatures range from 54 to 69°F. The baits are usually fished on a Bait Walker rig (right).

Notice I said frozen chicken livers. Some anglers may disagree, feeling that fresh liver is better, but a biologist I know says that freezing and thawing liver releases a surge of fish-attracting amino acids. Plus, frozen liver stays on the hook much better.

Blue cats often prefer rotten or decaying bait. However, during spring, try using fresh cut bait such as shad, suckers or chubs. Frogs, leeches or salamanders also take blue and channel cats when spring overlaps summer and water temperatures range from 68 to 76°F.

Dip baits work best on these two species after the water reaches 72°F, and really produces at higher water temperatures (78 to 84°F).

Where Do They Go?

After the spring feeding binge, catfish do a disappearing act, leaving anglers confused and frustrated. Once the water warms into the low 70s, they move away from the dam and begin looking for nesting sites. Channels and blues are sticklers for cover. They spawn in hollow logs, sunken barrels, undercut banks, muskrat burrows, natural cavities, bluff banks or brush piles.

Head for cover once the water warms; that's where you'll find cats.

Rig cut shad, chicken liver or nightcrawlers on a 3/0 hook tied to a 30-inch leader behind a 2-ounce Bait Walker sinker.

STRAIGHTLINING "TAP-TAP" CATS

During the cool water conditions of spring, channel cats hit a bait hard. Don't bother to let them run before setting the hook.

But once the water temperature exceeds the 70°F mark, hooking cats can be much tougher because they tend to "tap-tap-tap" your bait. No matter how long you let them run, the hook comes in empty. Here's why this happens:

Years ago, I discovered that channel cats tend to work upstream after mouthing a bait. Once positioned upstream from the point of contact, often a distance of a foot or two, the cat crushes the bait and opens its mouth to inhale it. Then, with its mouth still open, the fish retreats back downstream. When it reaches the point where the bait was first inhaled, the cat turns right or left to search out another scent trail and more food.

I once observed this strange feeding technique in a man-made pond. After seeing that behavior, I devised a technique I call straightlining, which helps me hook upwards of 95 percent of those "tap-tap" cat-

Bobber Anne used chicken liver to take this 25-pound blue.

fish. How does straightlining work?

Using a Bait Walker rig (p. 73), cast directly downstream. Once the bait and sinker have settled to the bottom, tighten up until the sinker stands upright and your line becomes taut.

When a catfish inhales your bait and moves forward, the wire sinker pivots and the line at your rodtip goes slack. Get ready to set the hook!

Count one—two—three, then set the hook. Hard. You haven't felt a thing, but at this very moment the cat is crushing your bait with a closed mouth and is most vulnerable to being hooked.

If you wait longer, the cat will begin to back off with an open mouth and your now-crushed bait lying in it. When the fish returns to its original pickup point, it will turn sideways, mouth still open, and you feel the familiar tap-tap. Trouble is, it's too late! You will miss the fish more than 50 percent of the time if you set the hook now.

Believe me, straightlining is the only way to go when water temperatures exceed that 70°F mark.

An old-time cat angler once told me that all it takes to hook a few kitties is a bit of line, a few hooks and a couple of lead weights. That's often true, but there are times when cats are every bit as challenging as the smartest bass, and they'll tear up tackle like big rockfish or muskies.

That's why I'm a dedicated catman, and always will be.

Gapen's Straightlining Method

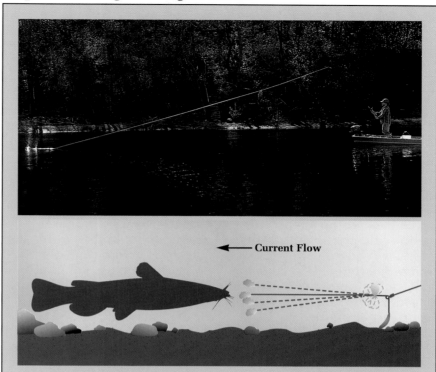

Cast downstream. Let the rig sink to the bottom and then tighten up the line to make the Bait Walker stand upright. Place your rod in a rod holder.

When a catfish starts tapping the bait, the sinker will lean back and your line will slacken. Pick up the rod, count to three and then set the hook.

ODORIFEROUS OFFERINGS

by Chris Altman & Jim Niemiec

Walk into a catfish-country bait shop on a hot summer's day and the odor will stop you in your tracks. You'd swear that something crawled into the walls and died. But you realize what's happening when you spot a couple of catmen in the back of the shop sniffing the selection of stinkbaits.

You can buy a variety of commercially made stinkbaits (also called prepared baits), or you can make your own "sour bait" from decomposed animal parts. The commercial products are a lot more convenient, but they may not have as much scent appeal as ripe fish or chicken parts.

Stinkbaits and sour baits are most commonly used for channels cats, but they also work well for smaller blues. Rarely, however, will these baits take a flathead or any very large catfish.

But some types of smelly baits do appeal to big cats, most notably super-oily salt-water baitfish such as mackerel, bonito and skipjack. While difficult for many inland anglers to obtain, these baits are a favorite of many trophy catfish specialists.

To an angler's nose, blood baits and fresh liver may not have an offensive smell, but as far as catfish are concerned, these baits have a super-intense scent that cannot be duplicated by any prepared bait. Congealed blood baits work well for all sizes of catfish, including giant blues. Methods for rigging and fishing blood bait are shown on pp. 67-69.

PREPARED BAITS

Prepared baits are categorized according to their consistency. Dip baits are made of runny goo into which you dip a hook with a piece of sponge to soak up the scent. Dough baits are stiff enough that they can be molded around a hook; they will last for hours before they dissolve. Paste baits are intermediate in consistency. They are often smeared on soft-plastic ringworms or squeezed into specially designed "tube baits" (p. 80) that allow them to ooze into the water.

Strong-smelling cheeses (such as limburger, garlic or sharp cheddar) also make good catfish bait. You can mix these baits with flour to stiffen them up (p. 81).

SOUR BAITS

Pieces of smelly, putrid fish make surprisingly good catfish bait in early spring. Fish that died during the winter decompose only slightly in the icy waters; but once the water begins to warm, decomposition proceeds rapidly. This explains why catfish feed more heavily on rotting fish in early spring than at any other time, and why ripe fish flesh makes such good springtime bait.

To duplicate the natural fare, anglers put 2- to 3-inch-wide strips of rough fish (such as carp or sheepshead) into a jar of water, seal it and then set it in the sun to ripen for a few days.

Many catmen swear by ripened chicken parts, including the entrails, but putrid flesh from most any other kind of animal will also attract cats.

SMELLY BAITFISH

Catfish anglers have long recognized the value of smelly baitfish such as shad and herring. Some anglers use these baits whole, but more often they are scaled and cut into chunks so they emit more odor into the water (p. 82).

In coastal areas, many catfishermen have access to oily saltwater baitfish such as mackerel, bonito and skipjack; these are are even smellier than the aforementioned freshwater baitfish. These saltwater baits are gaining in popularity as anglers in other parts of the country discover their cat-catching merits.

Some regional bait distributors now carry several types of frozen saltwater baitfish, and some bait shops are arranging to have them flown in from coastal areas.

Greenback mackerel have accounted for more giant California cats than any other bait. Their scent is strong enough that some anglers use a little mackerel oil to form a slick around the boat that attracts catfish and puts them in a feeding mood. The main drawback to mackerel is that the flesh breaks down rapidly, making it difficult to keep on the hook.

Bonito are closely related to tuna. They are much hard-

Popular prepared baits include: (1) Berkley PowerBait and (2) Berkley Power Paste, (3) LineBuster prepared cut bait, (4) Fish attractor scent and (5) dip bait.

er to come by than mackerel, but some say they are even better bait. The flesh of a bonito is a darker red and it contains more oil. Bonito stays on the hook better than mackerel and if you don't use it all, it can be refrozen for a later outing.

Perhaps the most sought-after bait by professional cat-men is the skipjack, not to be confused with skipjack her-ring, a popular freshwater cat-fish bait.

Skipjack, a member of the tuna family, is caught in blue water off both coasts and in the Gulf of Mexico. The meat of a skipjack is blood red and has an extremely fishy odor.

The skin is very tough and the flesh stays on the hook for hours.

These baits are normally cut into chunks and fished on a typical 2- or 3-hook cut-bait rig (p. 38) with size 1 hooks. For big cats, most anglers prefer larger bait chunks on an egg-sinker rig with size 1/0 hooks.

BLOOD/LIVER BAITS

You can make your own blood bait using beef blood or chicken blood obtained from slaughterhouses or processing plants, but many anglers pre-fer to order commercial blood

products which usually have a "secret ingredient" or some type of binder to help keep it on the hook. However, most veteran catfishermen believe that it's impossible to improve on the real thing.

Perhaps the best known of all catfish baits is chicken liver. It's easy to find and inexpensive, and it emits a bloody smell that has a spe-cial appeal to catfish. Beef liver also works well.

If you tend to have a weak stomach, these smelly baits may not be for you. Otherwise, put on some rubber gloves and bait up; to catfish, these baits smell like roses.

Popular Saltwater Baitfish

Greenback mackerel have an elongated shape with a metallic greenish or bluish color on the back, silvery undersides and irregular black stripes across the upper part of the body. The two dorsal fins are widely separated. The flesh of a mackerel is whitish.

Bonito have a deeper body than a mackerel with a metallic blue back, silvery undersides and 8 to 10 parallel black stripes on the sides that slope upward. The two dorsal fins are nearly joined at the base and the front dorsal has more than 16 spines. The flesh of a bonito is reddish.

Skipjack resemble bonito but their body is a little deeper and there are about 4 parallel black stripes on the lower half of the body. Skipjack are dark blue in color with a metallic sheen on the back; the undersides are silvery to dirty white. The two dorsal fins are nearly joined at the base, and the front dorsal has less than 16 spines. The flesh of a skipjack is blood red.

Smear paste bait onto a soft-plastic "ringworm." The ridges in the plastic help hold the bait in place.

Squeeze paste bait into a soft-plastic tube bait that has enough slits cut in it to allow the bait to slowly dissolve into the water. Thread your line through the tube and tie on a treble hook.

Form paste baits, dough baits, cheese baits, blood baits or chicken liver around a treble hook with a wire coil to help hold them in place.

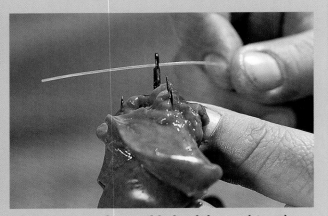

Rig liver on a plain treble hook by pushing the eye through a piece of liver and then pushing it onto each of the three points. When the bait is secure, tie your line to the hook.

Wrap delicate baits such as chicken livers, entrails or putrefied fish in a mesh bag made from a nylon stocking or piece of cheesecloth. Push a single hook through the bag.

Push a piece of sponge onto a treble hook and then immerse it in some dip bait. After 20 to 30 minutes of using this bait, reel in and dip it again to freshen it up!

Stinkbaiting Tips

Place several dozen small minnows, a few sliced shad or several carp fillets into a wide-mouth jar (left) and cover loosely. Put the jar in a sunny spot for a few days while the fish decomposes. When only an oily liquid remains, the potion is ready. Then put ¹/₂-inch cubes of sponge into the jar (right), screw the lid on tightly, shake the jar for a few minutes and let the sponges soak in the solution until ready to use. When fishing, put on a new sponge every 30 minutes or so and put the old one back into the jar.

Make cheese balls by mixing ¹/₂ pound of strong, finely grated cheese with 4 cups flour. Add just enough water to make a stiff dough. If desired, add a few teaspoons of anise oil, vanilla extract or angling scent. Form the dough into balls of the desired size and let dry (outside) for one or two hours. Then drop the doughballs into boiling water (left), cook them for about 30 minutes and remove them. After they dry, refrigerate them in a sealable plastic bag (right) for later use.

Make a catfish "cheeseburger" using equal parts of raw hamburger and a strong cheese like limburger. Mix with hot water and enough flour so the mixture will form balls that stay on the hook.

Drop a chunk of beef liver into a pot of boiling water for a minute or so; this stiffens it up enough so it will stay on the hook.

How to Prepare & Hook Cut Bait

Scale the whole, ungutted fish using a fish scaler or a large spoon, scraping from the tail toward the head.

Cut off the head and then slice the rest of the body into ³/₄-inch-thick steaks, discarding the tail section. Or filet the fish as shown on page 131.

Hook the head by pushing the hook into the mouth and out the top of the skull.

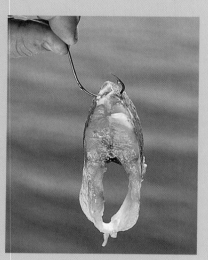

Hook a steak by pushing the hook through one side of the back and out the other. Make sure the hook penetrates the skin.

Hook a filet or a skin-on strip by pushing the hook through the skin and out the "meat" side.

Thread the entrails of a shad or other smelly baitfish onto a hook, just as if you were hooking a gob of nightcrawlers.

"Fly Lining" with Smelly Cut Bait

by Jim Niemiec

"Fly lining" is the hottest new catfishing technique among lake and pond catfishermen in the West. But don't get the idea that cats have suddenly started slurping dry flies off the surface like trout. Fly lining actually means presenting smelly, unweighted cut bait on a plain hook with a spinning outfit. The bait then settles slowly, like a subsurface fly, drawing the attention of foraging cats.

Slow-sinking cut bait has a near-magical appeal to catfish.

There are times when catfish will feed just like some types of saltwater gamefish. They push baitfish up to the surface and start to feed aggressively in a boiling topwater frenzy. That's the time to grab a rod rigged for fly lining.

Rigging Up

The basic outfit used in fly lining for catfish is a 7-foot medium-power graphite spinning rod and a spinning reel with a smooth drag and a capacity of about 150 yards of 20-pound-test mono. Some anglers prefer fluorescent line for fly lining at night because it's more visible than ordinary mono, especially when illuminated with a black light.

The only terminal tackle you'll need is a selection of laser-sharpened bait hooks in sizes 4 to 5/0.

The Best Baits

Most western fly liners fish with mackerel, but most any kind of smelly cut bait will do the job. Because you're not using a sinker, you'll need a decent-sized chunk of bait to provide casting weight. Most fishermen use a piece about the size of a half dollar, but anglers fishing for giant blues (50- to 80-pounders) often use half a mackerel on a size 7/0 hook.

The Basic Technique

Hit the water about 10 p.m. on a warm, windless evening and plan to stay until about 2 a.m. Head for a quiet cove away from other boaters or shore fishermen. Shut off the engine, turn off any deck lights (leave running lights on) and begin a drift with the breeze. When night-feeding catfish start to become active, you will hear splashes as smaller catfish begin to break up schools of shad. The larger trophy catfish are not nearly as active; they just hang around and pick off the leftovers.

If you cannot see splashes or ripples on the surface, quietly move the boat in the direction of the noise until you spot fish boiling. The bite may be slow at first, but a few little ripples can develop into an explosive feeding frenzy when schools of hungry catfish move in.

When you drift into casting range, stop the boat, cast right into the middle of the biggest boil you see and let the cut bait sink. Keep your bail open and feed line so the bait sinks straight down.

What happens next is critical to hooking a catfish. Watch the line as it comes off the reel. If you see it speed up, a catfish has picked up the bait and is swimming off. Don't be in a hurry to set the hook; sometimes a fish will spit the bait and then come back and pick it up again. Let the fish run off 15 to 20 feet of line. Then set the hook as hard as you can, bringing the rod way over your head to pick up any slack line caused by the fish doubling back or not swimming off in a straight line.

Once you hook a fish, play it for a while to determine its size and whether or not you need a light to land it. If it's a big fish, turn on the lights, clear the deck and grab a big landing net. If it's a small cat, just haul it into the boat without a net; this way the lights won't foul up your night vision.

But you don't necessarily have to do your fly lining at night. When on the prowl for food during the day, catfish often drive their prey onto rocky points, push them up against concrete dam faces or corner them in the back ends of coves. You can use the fly lining technique in any of these situations.

TROTLINE TACTICS

by Chris Altman

Some would argue that trotlining is more of a commercial-fishing method than a sport, but nobody would disagree that it is the most productive technique for catching catfish on hook and line.

For those not familiar with the method, a trotline is a long line rigged with numerous baited hooks. It is stretched across an area suspected to hold catfish, usually just before sundown, then checked sometime the next morning.

Catfish feed heavily at night and hook themselves when they take the bait. All the fisherman has to do is pull in the line and remove the fish.

TROTLINE CONSTRUCTION

A trotline consists of a main line to which are connected numerous droplines,

each with a hook at the end. All lines should be made of synthetic material such as nylon or polypropylene, so they won't rot.

Some catfishermen use a main line as light as 250-pound test, but a heavier line (at least 600-pound test) works better because its larger diameter is easier on the hands. The length of the main line varies with the size of the area to be covered and the number of hooks you want to use. Most trotlines are 100 to 250 feet long.

Droplines are normally 12 to 24 inches long and made of 100-pound-test line. A "hanging loop" dropline (below) is best for attaching hooks and changing them quickly.

A hanging loop not only gives you a stronger connection than you would get with a knot, it enables you to easily replace a damaged hook without cutting and shortening your dropper.

The droplines should be attached to the main line using barrel swivels. When catfish are hooked, they twist and turn trying to free themselves. Without swivels, they would spin around on the dropper, eventually wrapping it into a tight ball and getting enough leverage to free themselves. The swivels should not be tied to the main line, but held in place with crimp-on metal stops (below). This way, a fish cannot wrap the dropper around the main line and pull free.

Hook size depends mainly on the size of your bait. Most trotliners prefer size 2/0 to 5/0 forged, heavy-duty hooks. Long-shank hooks are best because they are easier to remove should a fish swallow the bait. Stainless-steel hooks will not corrode, so they last longer than ordinary steel hooks.

How to Make a Trotline

1 *Slip large barrel swivels onto the main line and secure them at 2- to 4-foot intervals using crimp-on metal stops available at net-supply houses.*

2 *Tie a dropper to each barrel swivel. If you want an 18-inch dropper, use a 36-inch piece of line and double it.*

3 *Attach a hook by slipping the dropper loop through the eye and then pushing the hook point through the loop. Tie an overhand knot in the dropper a few inches above the hook.*

TROTLINE BAITS

Trotliners bait up with everything from Ivory soap to dead ground squirrels, but certain baits lend themselves to trotlining better than others.

Most trotline anglers prefer a tough bait that cannot be easily pulled off the hook. Cut bait from bluegills, carp, suckers, herring or shad, for example, is a better choice than a soft bait like congealed blood or chicken livers. Catfish often pick the hooks clean of soft bait without hooking themselves.

Hardy live baits like bluegills, creek chubs or suckers are also popular among trotliners, especially where there is a good chance of encountering flatheads.

Many trotliners regard catalpa worms as one of the finest catfish baits. These black-and-yellow caterpillars exude a smell that cats find irresistible. It's not unusual to catch cats on bare hooks that were previously baited with catalpa worms. Other good baits include nightcrawlers, and whole crayfish or their peeled-tail sections.

SETTING A TROTLINE

Trotlining success depends largely on placing your line in the right location. If you are familiar with the body of water you're fishing, finding a good trotlining spot should not be difficult. The trick is to keep moving your line until you start catching good numbers of cats.

In a small river or stream, trotlines are normally strung from bank to bank. This way you have a good chance of intercepting any cats moving up or down the channel.

In a large river, where it would be impossible to cover the entire width, tie one end of the trotline to the bank and run the other end out into the river.

If possible, attach one end of the line to a flexible object that can provide some "give" to the line. A tree branch, for example, will act

Prime Trotlining Locations in Rivers

Trotline for river catfish in (1) tailraces, (2) deep pools, (3) eddies and (4) below tributaries. In the latter, run your line so it parallels the bank immediately downstream of the inflow.

as a shock absorber, preventing a big cat from gaining too much leverage and breaking a dropper line or straightening a hook.

Be sure to set your trotline to cover any areas where catfish concentrate such as deep pools, tailraces and areas below tributaries.

In streams or reservoirs that are not thermally stratified, weight your trotline so the hooks are on the bottom. Weights include everything from bricks to old window weights.

In stratified reservoirs you may catch more cats by keeping your line well above the bottom using floating jugs (p. 88). In impoundments that

harbor blue cats, trotlines are often fished only a few feet below the surface to catch blues that are following enormous schools of shad and herring.

Reservoir cats are normally found in the main river channel or creek channels, along channel breaks or other sharp ledges, around rock piles and humps and along any riprap banks such as dam, road and bridge facings. As a rule, any structure that has a hard rocky bottom and a sharp drop into deep water has potential to hold catfish.

Because most of the forage in any body of water is found in the shallows, that's where

savvy catmen do most of their trotlining. Shallow lines are especially effective after dark, when large numbers of cats move into water only a few feet deep to feast on the super-abundant forage.

But if you're intent on catching giant catfish, set your trotlines in deep water. The largest catfish seldom leave their deep-water haunts.

It's not surprising that so many catfishermen enjoy trotlining. There's a certain aura of excitement when you pull up the line, because there's always the possibility that you soon could be tangling with the cat of a lifetime.

Prime Trotlining Locations in Reservoirs

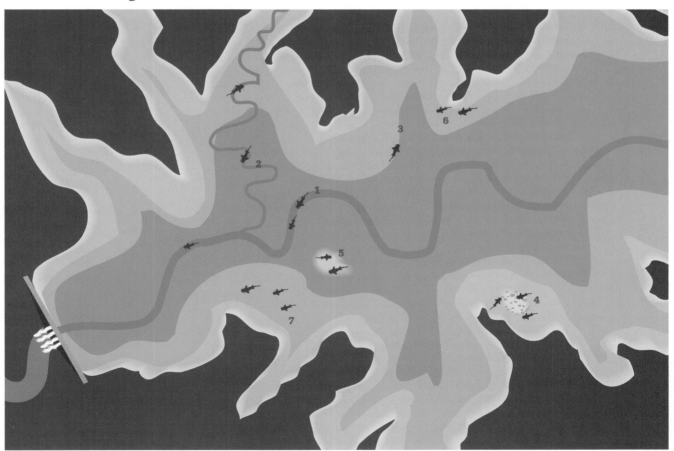

Trotline for reservoir cats in (1) the main river channel, (2) creek channel, (3) along any sharp ledges, around (4) rock piles and (5) humps, and on (6) points and (7) flats.

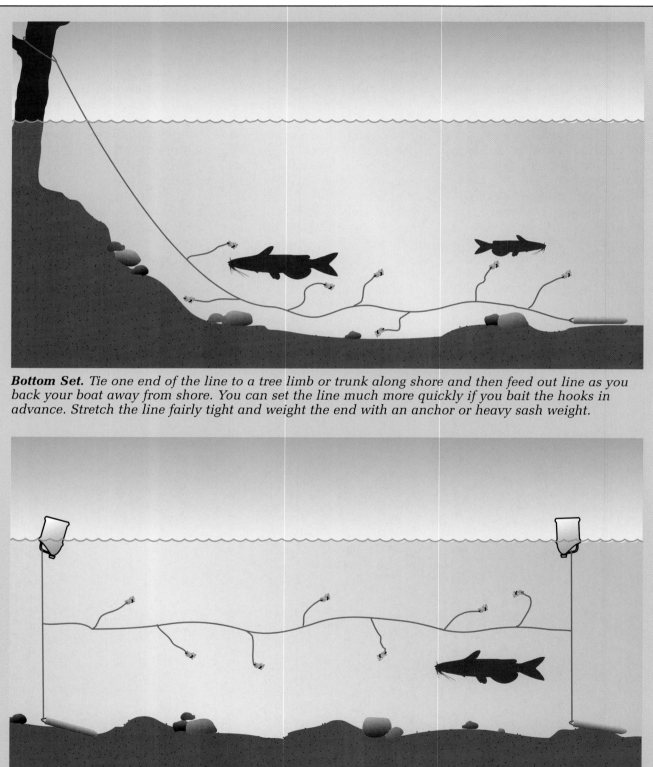

Bottom Set. *Tie one end of the line to a tree limb or trunk along shore and then feed out line as you back your boat away from shore. You can set the line much more quickly if you bait the hooks in advance. Stretch the line fairly tight and weight the end with an anchor or heavy sash weight.*

Floating Set. *Make an H-shaped set by stretching your trotline between two vertical cords with a plastic jug on one end and an anchor on the other. On a long line, use another jug on a cord to hold up the middle section.*

Gathering Catalpa Worms

Look for catalpa worms on the leaves of catalpa trees, which are easy to identify by their large heart-shaped leaves. The worms are normally found from late spring through early fall.

Spread a sheet on the ground and shake the catalpa limbs to collect the worms. Freeze them in plastic bags for use later in the year.

Three Trotlining Tips

Make a trotline from a kit containing all the components: main line, dropper line, hooks and swivels.

To avoid tangling, set your line from a specially-made trotline box consisting of a tray for the main line and slots to hold the droppers.

Run a trotline by pulling yourself along the main line, netting catfish as you go. If you attempt to hoist a large cat into the boat using the dropper, the hook may tear out. If you plan on fishing again soon, just leave the line in the water but don't bait it until late in the day.

"BUSH"-WHACKING CATFISH

by Chris Altman

To some catfishermen, nothing causes a surge of adrenaline like a twig bouncing on the water. It's a visual signal that a cat has grabbed your limbline.

A limbline (also called a bush-hook) consists of nothing more than a hook and a short piece of twine tied to a tree limb. But it may just be the the most formidable weapon ever conceived in the annals of catfishing.

According to veteran catman Frank Billiter, "The only technique in the world that will even come close to the productivity of bush-hooks is graveling (catching spawning cats by hand). When compared to trotlines ... well, there is no comparison. Bush-hooks provide more hook and bait control; you can position the bait exactly where the catfish feed; and you can position it in such a way that they are almost always hooked when they take the bait. And once hooked, the fish rarely pull off of the line."

THE BASIC RIG

A limbline consists of a quality hook (size 2/0 wide-gap) tied to a 4- to 6-foot piece of strong twine (100-pound-test bonded nylon). Bonded line will not unravel like normal nylon twine.

Simply bait up with a lively minnow and tie the line to a small, green limb hanging over the water.

Most anglers position their bait within a foot or so of the surface. Others, however, prefer to let the bait ride barely beneath the surface where it causes more commotion as it struggles to free itself. Often the eye of the hook actually sticks out of the water.

Tie your line to a small limb that is green and supple. This way, it will bend and give as a cat fights against it. A stout limb may break, or you may wind up with a broken line or straightened hook.

Most bush-hook fishermen prefer long limbs because they're more forgiving; a short limb may simply tear away from the tree.

Before tying your line to the tree limb, make sure the line is short enough so the hook cannot reach the bank or some obvious snag in the water. Otherwise a catfish could tangle the line or snag the hook and pull free.

How to Make & Set a Limbline

1 Tie a size 2 forged-steel hook to a piece of 100-pound-test bonded nylon twine. The hook should have an extra-large eye so the twine will fit through it. Burn the tag end to secure the knot.

2 Tie the line to a flexible limb so the bait is barely beneath the surface. Make sure the line is out of reach of the shoreline or any snags.

WHEN AND WHERE TO FISH A LIMBLINE

Most experts agree the best time for running limblines is in late spring and early summer, when cats are preparing to spawn. Then the fish are generally in shallow water where a limbline can be effective.

Limblines also catch cats immediately following the spawning period, and they may even work in summer and fall. In the southern U.S., where temperatures remain moderate throughout the winter, limblining can be a year-round sport.

Like trotlines, limblines are usually set before sunset and checked the next morning. Catfish that move into the shallows to feed at night quickly detect the struggling baitfish.

Frank Billiter recommends setting limblines along shallow stretches of the bank. "When we set bush-hooks down a length of riverbank, we'll catch four times as many fish from shallow water as we will from the deeper pools," he says. "For one thing, I don't really believe that a baitfish struggling on the surface 15 feet or more above the catfish will attract much attention—

it's just too far away. We always set our bush-hooks in water less than 10 feet deep."

While most limblining is done in shallow stretches of small to medium-sized rivers, limblines are also effective in the upper ends of many impoundments, where the water is relatively shallow and there is a noticeable current.

Good limblining locations include the upper ends of pools and any gravel bars adjacent to deep water. Large flats are seldom good producers. Limblines set along steep banks, especially those that are undercut, are usually bet-

Where to Set Limblines

Good limblining locations include: (1) pool or deep slot below a tributary stream, which serves as a combination feeding and resting area; (2) upper end of a deep pool (close to the bank if possible), where catfish can easily intercept drifting food; (3) logjam or other woody cover, which makes a prime

ter than limblines set along shallow, gradually sloping shorelines. Rocky bluffs are superb limblining locations, as are tributaries flowing in just upstream from a deep hole.

When scouting for flatheads, be on the lookout for logjams or other woody cover.

LIMBLINING BAITS

"We don't bait our bushhooks with anything but freshly-caught live bait," says Billiter. "Our favorite for catching a bunch of eatingsized cats is a 2- to 3-inch chub. But when we're hunting big cats, we prefer 6- to 8-inch chubs, suckers or even small catfish. Cats are cannibalistic, so smaller cats and madtoms are also great baits."

Silver-dollar-sized bluegills also work well on a limbline. These hardy little fish will swim on the surface for hours. If you're intent on catching a bruiser cat, don't be afraid to try suckers or chubs up to a foot long. Another good choice is an 8- to 10-inch carp.

Some say that limblining is not much of a sport, but when you pull up to a tree and see that limb dancing, you can't help but get excited.

Limblining Baits

Good limblining baits include small bluegills (1) and catfish (2), 8- to 10-inch carp (3), and suckers (4) or chubs (5) up to a foot long.

resting area; and (4) steep, undercut banks, which offer both shade and overhead cover.

Trotlining and Limblining: The Legalities

Before doing any trotlining or limblining, be sure to check your state's laws regarding these activities. There may be restrictions on which waters you can fish, how many hooks you can use, length of your trotline, etc. In some states, you may even have to buy a commercial fishing license.

Many states require that each limbline and trotline be labeled with your name, address and phone number.

Be sure to check your trotlines and limblines each day, and remove them from the water when they will not be used for a period of time. Otherwise they may continue to catch and kill catfish and other types of gamefish.

JUGGIN' SUMMERTIME CATS

by Chris Altman

The easiest, most relaxing and (at times) most productive catfishing technique is drifting a bait under a plastic jug. The method can be used during much of the year, but is most effective in summer, when catfish suspend in thermally stratified bodies of water.

In summer, most lakes and ponds stratify into three temperature layers: the epilimnion; the metalimnion or thermocline; and the hypolimnion (see below). Because the hypolimnion often is short of oxygen during the summer months, catfish are restricted to the upper layers and tend to spend most of their time in or just above the thermocline.

In most larger impoundments, the thermocline begins some 15 to 25 feet below the surface. In smaller ponds, however, the thermocline may be considerably shallower, beginning only 5 or 6 feet down.

At times you can easily determine the bounds of the thermocline using your electronics. Plankton often concentrates in the thermocline and appears as a vague band on a liquid-crystal or video graph. This band can be seen most anywhere on the lake.

But if the plankton layer is not present, you'll need an electric thermometer to find the thermocline. Simply lower the probe until the water temperature begins dropping rapidly (about half a degree per foot). When the probe goes below the thermocline, the temperature continues falling but at a much slower rate.

Because catfish in a stratified impoundment suspend on the thermocline just as if it were a physical structure, many anglers have trouble locating and catching them. Catfish suspending just over the thermocline could be anywhere in the lake, and finding them is a time-consuming process. That's where jug fishing comes in.

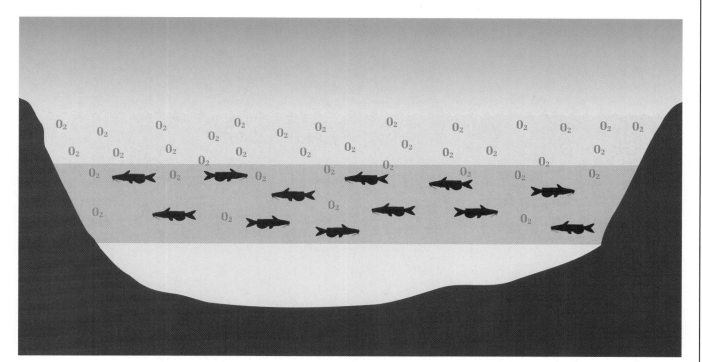

Most man-made lakes, natural lakes and ponds form three distinct temperature layers in summer. The warmer, lighter water in the epilimnion (pink) stays on top of the colder, denser water. It is easily circulated by the wind, so it stays well-oxygenated. The water in the hypolimnion (blue) does not circulate, so it gradually loses oxygen as the summer progresses. Catfish are commonly found in the thermocline (purple), where there is adequate oxygen and a moderate water temperature, although they often move into the epilimnion to feed, especially at night.

JUGS & HOW TO RIG THEM

Catfishing jugs can be made from virtually any plastic container. The most important consideration is size of the jug. Many think a small jug (like a quart oil bottle) is too small to wear down a big cat. That may be true if you hook a monstrous cat, but an oil bottle will eventually tire even a cat in the 15- to 30-pound range. The fish may pull the jug under for several minutes and it may pop up again more than 100 feet away; but if the line doesn't tangle in a snag, you should be able to land the fish. One big advantage to smaller jugs: they don't take up much room in the boat. A big disadvantage is that they may be difficult to see on a large expanse of water.

If there's a chance of hooking giant catfish, rig up larger jugs, such as gallon milk jugs, antifreeze containers or 2-liter pop bottles.

Some fishermen use 30 jugs or more, but that makes for a lot of work. A more reasonable number is 15 to 20 jugs per angler.

JUG-FISHING BASICS

The majority of jug fishing takes place at night. Not only are catfish nocturnal, the jugs pose a hazard to water skiers and other daytime boaters. And in many waters, gar will pick your hooks clean if you set your jugs during the day.

After you determine the right depth, adjust your jug lines accordingly. Many jug fishermen set their lines to fish a little above the thermocline, because catfish do not hesitate to swim up to grab a bait. Shallow lines work especially well for blue cats; they feed at any depth where there is adequate oxygen, and they don't hesitate to swim all the way to the surface to find food.

Bait jug lines with virtually any kind of proven catfish bait, alive or dead. Live baits such as creek chubs and bluegills are extremely hardy and will stay alive for long periods, even in warm water.

Cut bait from shad, herring, bluegills or even carp are also effective. But soft baits like chicken liver, congealed blood and most stinkbaits are not good choices, because small cats and other fish often pick the hooks clean.

There are two basic jug-fishing methods. You can set your jugs out and drift with them, keeping an eye on them for any sign of a bite. Or you can set the jugs out at sundown and then check them later in the evening or early the next morning. The

How to Make Catfishing Jugs

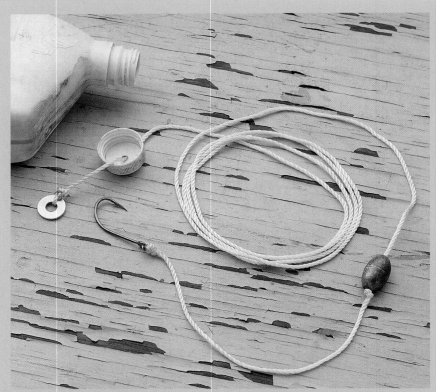

To make a catfishing jug from a one-quart plastic oil bottle, drill a small hole through the lid and run a piece of nylon cord through the hole. Next, select a metal washer that will fit into the bottle's spout and tie it to the line extending inside the lid. Drop the washer into the bottle, screw on the lid and add a sinker and size 1/0 to 3/0 hook. A 1/2- to 2-ounce sinker is adequate for most jug fishing; it should be attached 18 to 24 inches above the hook. Live baits and long lines require heavier sinkers than do cut bait and short lines.

latter method is obviously the easiest, but the former enables you to catch more fish. And it is the only effective way to fish jugs in a river or stream.

In a lake, the usual strategy is to drop your baited rigs on the upwind side and allow the wind to carry them to the downwind shore. By selecting the lake's widest spot, you can cover the most water with the least effort. Of course, you may have trouble locating all your jugs in the morning.

When a catfish takes the bait, it may pull the jug under momentarily. Or the jug may bob a little and then settle to rest. So there may be a fish on the line even if the jug is not moving.

When you pick up a jug, lift it gently to see if there is a fish on it. If you feel extra weight, pull the line in hand over hand. If it's a large fish, be sure to use a landing net; the hook may tear out if you try to hoist it in.

Once the water begins to cool in fall, the lake turns over, restoring oxygen to all depths. Cats can now go wherever they want and may be found at a variety of depths. Consequently, jug fishing is not nearly as effective as it was when the lake was stratified.

Before doing any jug fishing, be sure to check your state's regulations. Some states limit the number of jugs allowed per angler, and most require that anglers mark each jug with a name, address and phone number. In a few states, jug fishing is prohibited.

That's testimony to the effectiveness of the technique.

To make a jug from a two-liter pop bottle, tie your line around the bottle's neck. Because most pop bottles have a clear-plastic exterior, they must be painted to increase visibility.

H-shaped marker buoys may double as catfishing jugs. To adjust the depth, just tie a half hitch so the line can't unwind.

Gallon milk jugs with screw-on tops and antifreeze bottles make good catfishing jugs. Just tie the line to the molded handle.

Drifting jugs along a shallow, rocky streambank is a deadly catfishing method.

More Jug-Fishing Opportunities

Jugging is most effective in summer, when lakes are stratified into temperature layers. But it also works well in the pre- and post-spawn periods, when cats prowl the shallows. And during the spawn, jugs released along shallow, rocky or riprap banks will produce cats in both rivers and impoundments.

In small to mid-sized rivers, cats hold and feed in pools below shoals or, in the case of blue cats, in swift-water chutes. The most natural way to present a bait to these fish is to drift jugs through the feeding areas (below).

How to Fish Jugs in Streams

Anchor just upstream from the shoal and release a series of jugs. The current carries the jugs and your baits through the shoal and into the pool below.

After the jugs have drifted through the pool, retrieve them, motor back upstream and release them again. After two or three drifts through a shoal/pool area, move downstream to the next area and repeat the procedure.

Five Jug-Fishing Tips

Use a jug that is highly visible. Most jug fishermen prefer white, but yellow and fluorescent orange also show up quite well. If your jugs are not the right color, you can easily spray-paint them.

To retrieve your jugs after sundown, use a power-ful, hand-held spotlight. During the day, search for the jugs with the sun to your back to elimi-nate glare.

Use binoculars to locate jugs in open expanses of water.

Measure the length of the line and use a waterproof pen to write it on the jug. Then, when you're catching fish, you'll immediately know what depths are best so you can set the other lines accordingly.

To fish several baits on the same jug, tie surgeon's loops (p. 38) at 18-inch intervals from the end of the line. Then attach a leader and hook to each loop and add a sinker to the end of the line.

NOODLIN' CATS

by Don Wirth

Down in the hollows east of Bowling Green, Kentucky, mid-June is greeted with anticipation by a certain cult of outdoorsmen.

That's when noodlin' season opens on Barren River Lake.

This little-known form of angling, also known as graveling, ticklin' or hoggin',

involves wading the margins of streams and lakes, groping into holes and under submerged logs and rocks for big catfish. Noodlers feel for the

fish bare-handed, sticking their fingers or hands inside a cat's mouth and wrestling it ashore by brute force.

"Noodlin' time is something we really look forward to," says Gary Stinson of Scottsville, Kentucky. "We start preparing our holes in winter, when the lake is drawn down." Noodlers prop up big rocks with boards and smaller rocks to create "hides" (mini-caves) for catfish, usually flatheads, to spawn and hide in. Then, when the lake comes up and the water warms in late spring, the noodlers make their rounds. Often there's a catfish, sometimes two, in every hole.

Although most noodlin' involves hand-to-mouth combat, many Kentucky noodlers use a long hickory or oak staff with a shark hook on one end. The staff serves as a prod to find the fish and move it into position where it can be grabbed or hooked.

When a noodler locates a cat, he places a large rock to partially block the entrance to the hole, preventing the cat from escaping. If the hole is too deep to probe by hand, the cat can be located with the staff.

Stinson sometimes uses a technique called stringin', which is a variation of the basic noodlin' technique. "I'll feel around for the cat's head," Stinson explains, "you can tell it's a big one when your fingers can't touch its eyes when your hand is spanned. Then I'll poke my hand inside its mouth, take a barbless shark hook on a stout cord and run the hook through the cat's lip, just like I was putting the fish on a stringer. The cat often sits there calmly while all this is going on—if you do it just

right and don't get in too much of a hurry, that is. If it panics and bolts, you could get hurt."

Once the fish is strung, the noodler hangs on to the rope, unblocks the hole and the fish swims out. When the moving catfish pulls the slack out of the line, the battle begins. It might take two men to subdue a big flathead—one holding the rope and the other grabbing the fish under one arm while a free hand clenches it by the lower jaw. All of this takes place amidst much thrashing and splashing. "It's a real tug-of-war," Stinson laughs. "A big flathead will just about drown you!"

Noodlin' is every bit as risky as its sounds. Unless you grab the catfish just right, it might run a spiked fin (or the shark hook) clear through your hand. Broken or dislocated fingers are also a distinct possibility. Wrestling with a giant cat while standing on loose rocks often results in scrapes and ankle sprains; more than one

noodler has slipped, fallen and broken a leg or arm. It's even rumored that backcountry noodlers have been dragged into the depths by monster catfish they simply could not control.

Like skateboarding abrasions, skinned and bleeding fingers are considered badges of honor. Stinson's hands looked like raw hamburger after noodlin' over a hundred pounds of flatheads in just two hours. I asked him if he'd ever accidentally latched onto a cottonmouth or snapping turtle while noodlin'. "No, but I've grabbed a mud puppy [large aquatic salamander] a time or two," he replied.

Like buck dancing or playing a hammered dulcimer, noodlin' is a skill that's passed down through generations of country folk, one that's in danger of disappearing as the deeply-rural South slowly gets eaten up by the "civilized" world surrounding it.

Some noodlers wear swimming trunks so they can pull cats from deep-water hides.

THE BOOK ON BULLHEADS

by Dick Sternberg

When I was a kid, my daily summertime ritual consisted of digging up a handful of angleworms, hopping on my bike and heading for a shallow, muddy lake near my home to fish for bullheads.

One Saturday, I skipped confirmation class because the bullhead "bite" was really on. But when the preacher called to ask where I was, my dad knew right where to find me.

You don't read much about bullheads in the major fishing magazines, but the fish have a surprisingly large group of loyal followers. And it's easy to understand why: bullheads are found most everywhere, they're easy to catch and they're hard to beat on the dinner table.

BEST PLACES/TIMES

Practically all small, warmwater streams or shallow lakes, even those that periodically winterkill, hold a decent population of black bullheads. If you're specifically targeting brown or yellow bullheads, however, look for clearer, weedier lakes that are best known for walleyes, bass or panfish.

Bullheads are seldom caught in winter. But once the water starts to warm in spring, they begin moving into any shallow areas connected to the main lake or river. Look for them in backwater lakes, sloughs, canals, marinas and feeder creeks that are a few degrees warmer than the main body of water. If there are no connecting waters, you'll find springtime bullheads in the shallowest, warmest part of a lake or pond. In streams, they often congregate below low-head dams or other barriers to upstream migration.

Once spawning is completed, some bullheads (usually blacks) may stay put, but most of them move back to the main lake or river where they are much more difficult to find. As the summer progresses, however, the fish begin to congregate in weedy areas and along shallow structure.

Many anglers share the mistaken belief that bullheads are usually found on a soft, mucky bottom. In reality, they prefer a firm bottom and are found in mucky areas only when a firmer substrate is not available.

Bullheads can be caught most any time of the day, but they generally bite best starting at sunset and continuing until several hours after dark.

Summer bullhead locations in a lake: (1) shallow weedy hump, (2) point, (3) weedline, (4) sharp shoreline lip, (5) spawning bay.

Make a multiple-hook rig by splicing your line together with blood knots (left) spaced about a foot apart. To tie a blood knot, (1) hold the lines alongside each other, with the ends facing opposite directions; (2) wrap one line around the other 4-5 times, and pass the free end between the two lines, as shown; (3) repeat step 2 with the other line; (4) pull on both lines to snug up the knot. Trim only one tag end of each knot. The untrimmed tag ends should be 4-6 inches long. Tie a bell sinker to the end of the line and add a hook to each of the untrimmed tag ends (right). With the hooks ahead of the sinker, subtle bites will be easy to detect.

BULLHEAD BAITS/RIGS

You can catch bullheads on stinkbaits, dough baits, cheese baits, cut baits, blood baits or most any other kinds of baits that work well for catfish. But day in and day out, it's hard to beat a couple of garden worms or a nightcrawler on a size 2 to 1/0 hook.

It's important to use a hook with a long shank, because bullheads often swallow the bait.

The usual bottom-fishing rig consists merely of a hook with a pinch-on or Rubber-Cor sinker, but some anglers prefer a multiple-hook rig (above).

Some bullhead anglers prefer slip-sinker rigs, but they're seldom needed; once a bullhead grabs the bait, it's not likely to let go just because it feels a little resistance.

Although bullheads spend most of their time on the bottom, they suspend on occasion and sometimes hold over a thin layer of bottom vegeta-tion. Then a float rig is a better choice. You can get by with a clip-on or peg-on float in shallow water, but a slip-float is recommended for depths of 5 feet or more. Pinch on just enough split shot to balance the float.

Any medium-power spinning or baitcasting outfit spooled with 6- to 10-pound mono will do the job. In woody or brushy cover, however, some anglers opt for a medium-heavy baitcasting outfit with braided Dacron or superline as heavy as 30-pound-test. Bullheads aren't the least bit line-shy, so the heavy line will not reduce the number of bites.

FISHING METHODS

There's nothing complicated about bullhead fishing. Just toss out a bottom rig, prop your rod up on a forked stick or place it in a rod holder and wait for a bite. When you see a tap or tug on your rod tip, grab the rod, drop the tip back for a second or two to let the fish take the bait and then set the hook.

When float-fishing, try to keep your bait as close to the bottom or the weed tops as possible. When bullheads are feeding on the bottom, as they normally do, they're not inclined to swim up more than a few inches to take a bait.

Although jigs are not normally considered bullhead baits, a jig tipped with a piece of worm or a leech works surprisingly well for the angler who prefers casting to still-fishing.

You don't need fancy equipment to catch bullheads. There's not a whole lot of strategy involved, and the fish are almost always biting. So if you're into angling challenges, bullhead fishing is probably not for you. But if you just want to have a good time catching a mess of tasty fish, grab your pitchfork, head for the garden, dig up a can of worms, then go have some old-fashioned fun.

Bullhead-Fishing Tips

Use a floating jig head to keep your bait above a thin layer of vegetation or to keep it from settling into a mucky bottom where it would not be visible to the fish.

Pinch down your barb to make hook removal much easier. Then, should a bullhead swallow the bait, you can extract the hook in seconds and get your line back into the water.

Wrap a rubber band around your rod handle and slip a loop of line under it; this way you can tighten your line a little to easily detect bites, yet a slight tug will pull the line free so the fish won't feel too much resistance.

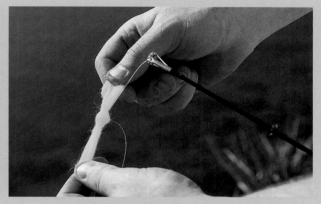

After securing the line with a rubber band (left), tie a piece of yarn around the line (using an overhand knot) to serve as a bite indicator. This way you'll easily be able to spot bites from a distance.

Carry a hook remover in case a bullhead swallows the bait. A slotted plastic "disgorger" will do the job, but some anglers prefer a hemostat or "Hook-out."

Grip a bullhead as shown to remove the hook, being careful to avoid getting poked by the pectoral or dorsal spines (arrows), which have a weak venom and can inflict a painful wound.

SPECIAL SITUATIONS

*H*ere's how to stay on top of your catfish game in special situations that call for special strategies, techniques and tactics.

SMALL RIVER FLATHEADS

by Jeff Samsel

Big rivers like the Missouri, Ohio and Mississippi are legendary for the monstrous cats they produce. But bigger isn't always better, according to Ted Ellenbecker a trophy flathead specialist from Sioux Falls, South Dakota. Ellenbecker prefers to fish jumbo cats in the smaller rivers that feed these massive flows.

Giant cats from any big river will move up feeder streams to take advantage of easy pickings from spawning forage fish and to escape powerful spring flows in the main river, Ellenbecker contends. He has caught and released dozens of huge flatheads in rivers only 50 to 100 feet across.

Smaller rivers offer the major advantage of being much more manageable, Ellenbecker points out. Big rivers have currents that can be dangerous, especially in spring. And those currents make it extremely difficult (or impossible) to anchor properly and keep baits near the bottom in good spots. Productive areas are also much easier to locate than they would be in a vast waterway.

Ellenbecker's favorite small rivers flow directly into the Missouri River in southeastern South Dakota. But he has taken his small-river approach on the road several times and found it to be effective in little-known waters flowing into other major rivers. Although every river is a little different, Ellenbecker's basic strategy remains the same.

WHAT TO LOOK FOR

Ellenbecker prefers a stream that pours into a major river no more than 30 miles downstream of a dam, or close to a series of wing dams or riprap banks on the big river. Preferably, the small stream should have a dam to limit the distance the cats can move upstream. With or without such a barrier, he typically focuses on the lower third of the river.

Small rivers don't necessarily have to be deep to hold big flatheads, Ellenbecker notes. Most of the river can average only 4 feet deep, as long as there are washout holes 10 or 12 feet deep below shoal areas and along outside bends.

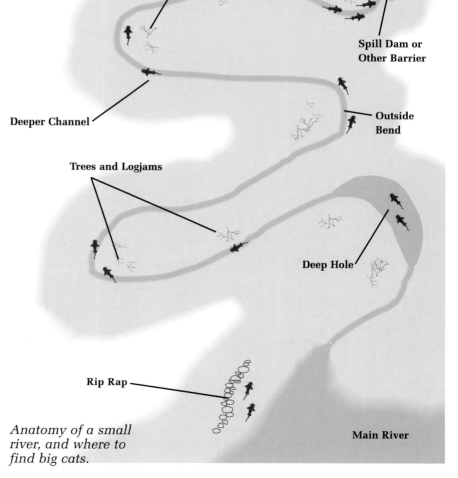

Any Woody Cover

Spill Dam or Other Barrier

Deeper Channel

Outside Bend

Trees and Logjams

Deep Hole

Rip Rap

Anatomy of a small river, and where to find big cats.

Main River

BAIT SELECTION

Ellenbecker uses live bait exclusively when he targets big flatheads, favoring wild creek chubs and suckers. "Wild," he stresses, is the key word. "Pond-reared baits just don't have the fight to attract big flatheads."

Most flathead veterans agree that live bait far out-produces any other kind of offering. Specific bait preferences vary dramatically depending on a river's natural forage species, baitfish types that anglers can catch or buy, and state fisheries laws governing legal baits. Some river fishermen will use gizzard shad up to 18 inches long or carp that weigh 3 pounds, but Ellenbecker prefers to stay a little smaller, even in summer when the cats need a lot of food.

"A 50-pound fish will hit an 8-inch bait," he explains, "and that bait also gives you the opportunity to catch a 10-pound flathead. I'm out there to have fun catching catfish, so I prefer a bait that any flathead will take."

SEASONAL STRATEGIES

Seasonal conditions cause cats to behave differently, Ellenbecker points out, so anglers need to change their methods depending on the time of year.

Early Season

Most catfish anglers believe flatheads don't bite in frigid water, but Ellenbecker begins catching them shortly after ice out.

In early season, however, heavy current makes large portions of any river off limits to flatheads, which favor slack water even more than other kinds of cats.

The flathead's penchant for slow water explains why the fish often move into smaller rivers and stack up behind current breaks, especially major structures like low-head dams.

Large numbers of big predators concentrated in small areas translate into heavy competition, explaining why they're feeding so aggressively despite the cold water. "The fish are concentrated and willing," Ellenbecker says.

Even so, flatheads favor a fairly small bait through early spring. Because their metabolic rate is low in the icy water, their food demands are small and they are less able to handle larger

Lower your bait into a logjam, lifting it slowly up and down to bump it off the cover. Keep your line as vertical as possible to minimize snagging. After thoroughly covering the spot, move downstream to the next logjam.

prey, Ellenbecker believes. A 4- to 6-inch live bait usually works better than an 8- to 10-inch. With a large bait, you would get fewer bites and hook a smaller percentage of the fish.

Late Spring/Summer

As the season progresses and water levels moderate, flatheads begin spreading through prime holding areas in small rivers, and fishing becomes more of a hunting game. Logjams, hard-bottom areas, deep holes, outside bends and current breaks all enter into the equation. To maximize his chances, Ellenbecker looks for spots that combine several of these elements.

"I look for a complex, with at least three elements in place," he explains. "Just a logjam or a deep hole is not enough. You'll find those all along the river."

The common denominator in every spot that Ellenbecker fishes is an abundance of woody cover, either right in the spot or close enough that the catfish can move easily to it. He noted that one South Dakota study showed catfish relating to woody cover up to 90 percent of the time.

During late spring and summer, Ellenbecker uses two different strategies, depending on the type of spot: "slipping timber" or "ambushing" the fish.

Slipping timber involves working your way down a river, probing potentially productive logjams for roughly 20 minutes apiece.

Ambushing means stillfishing in an area where you expect big cats to move through during the night.

Ellenbecker compares it to stand-hunting for deer.

To find a good ambush site, Ellenbecker looks for a major daytime resting area, such as a dense logjam near a deep hole He then seeks out a nearby nighttime feeding area, like a low-head dam or shallow flat, and sets up on a travel route between the two spots.

Determining the most likely travel route requires careful study of the river

bottom. If there is an unobstructed channel between the two spots, for example, catfish will follow it. Set up on the edge of the channel, closer to the feeding area than to the resting area, and position your boat so you can keep your bait right on the upper portion of the channel lip.

Most of Ellenbecker's largest flatheads, including one that missed the state record by only a couple

To locate small river flatheads, look for spots that concentrate or attract fish such as (1) a lowhead dam, (2) eddies just below the dam, (3) the upper lip of a wingdam and (4) a logjam in a hard-bottomed, slackwater zone.

pounds, were caught using this ambush strategy.

Fall

As summer gives way to fall, the water cools and cats begin feeding heavily in preparation for leaner times ahead. Throughout the fall, Ellenbecker focuses on deep holes below major current breaks, including wing dams and deep cuts in the bank. And because cats tend to migrate downstream in fall, he fishes almost exclusively within the lower 10 miles of a river's course.

Ellenbecker has found that fall fishing is usually best in morning or evening. It's also important to pick the right day. He prefers fishing when the weather is mild and has been that way for at least a few days.

The smaller baits that work well in spring are also effective for flatheads in late fall.

Whether he's fishing a current break in early season, slipping timber, or ambushing cats, Ellenbecker first checks out a potential fishing spot by making a few casts with only a sinker tied to his line. "That helps me locate the channels I should fish and snags I need to avoid. If I lose a sinker or two in a spot, I know not to go there," he explains.

RIGGING UP

Ellenbecker relies on the same rig for practically all of his fishing. Rather than using the traditional method of hooking live baitfish through the back, he hooks the bait (usually a chub or sucker) on the lower side of the body, near the tail. This keeps them swimming upright and off the bottom more effectively than the back-hooking method.

Ted Ellenbecker releases a nice flathead ... a mature fish that will live to breed—and be caught—again.

He normally uses a slip-sinker rig consisting of a 1- to 3-ounce bell sinker, a plastic bead, a heavy swivel, a piece of monofilament leader and, depending on the size of his bait, a 3/0 to 5/0 hook. His favorite hook is a heavy bronze, wide-gap Eagle Claw (model LO42).

Ellenbecker arms himself with heavy gear, so he's prepared when a trophy takes the bait. He prefers a stout 6½- to 7-foot muskie rod matched with an Ambassadeur 6500C reel.

For fishing tight to the timber, he spools up with 40-pound-test Berkley Big Game line. For fishing below a low-head dam or other snag-free area, he may drop down to 20-pound test, which works better in strong current because it has less drag.

Although Ellenbecker catches more than his share of giant cats, he is a conservationist at heart, releasing almost all his catfish. He has proposed regulations to restrict the harvest of large cats; although those regulations have not yet been implemented, the state has commissioned flathead research that could provide the scientific basis for such regulations in the future.

Ellenbecker has also initiated a public-awareness program to encourage other anglers to release larger fish. Signs have been posted at sites he believes are threatened by over-fishing; they point out that a 10-pound flathead is typically at least 10 years old. He does not say anglers should release all cats, he simply would like them to limit their take of large catfish to preserve the quality of future fishing. Good ideas in today's world.

Catch your own "wild" chubs and suckers in small creeks. All you need is an ultralight spinning outfit with 2-pound-test mono, a split shot and a size 12 hook baited with a piece of garden worm. As you catch the baitfish, put them in a flow-through minnow bucket.

Hook a sucker or chub by pushing a size 3/0 to 5/0 hook through the lower part of the tail.

SMALL-POND CATS

By Chris Altman

Being one of the most adaptable freshwater gamefish, catfish can live in most any kind of warmwater environment, save waters that are highly polluted. So it should come as no surprise that hundreds of thousands of small ponds across North America are good catfish producers. What may surprise many anglers, however, is the fact that such small waters produce such big cats.

The majority of small ponds are stocked with chan- nel cats, although white cats are rapidly gaining in popularity, mainly because they bite willingly in day- light hours. Blues may also thrive in a pond environ- ment, but flatheads do not fare as well.

TYPES OF PONDS

Although some ponds are just small natural lakes, the majority are created by man, either by damming a natural waterway or bulldozing a depression in the ground. Ponds are generally built for watering livestock, providing water for irrigation or controlling erosion, but some are created primarily for fishing.

Ponds built by damming a stream differ considerably from bulldozed or natural ponds (right), and those differences are important in planning your fishing strategy.

Dammed ponds usually have a steady flow of water passing through them, either from a small creek or from springs. If the flow is great enough, the water will be thoroughly mixed, so the pond will not stratify into distinct temperature layers. This means that catfish can be found at any depth, in summer or in winter.

Bulldozed ponds, however, are usually fed by surface runoff rather than a steady flow from a stream or spring. As a result, there is not enough mixing to prevent temperature layers from forming. The layer of stagnant water that develops on the bottom is low in oxygen, so it is off limits to catfish in midsummer and winter. Dammed ponds that have a minimal flow may also lack oxygen in the depths.

In recent years, fee-fishing ponds have become extremely popular. Catfish are periodically stocked and anglers pay a daily or per-fish fee.

CATFISH LOCATION IN PONDS

As a rule, catfish will congregate in the deepest holes in any pond. Look for fish in the central hole, the trench at the base of the dam or the old creek channel. These deep holes also serve as wintering areas, holding dense concentrations of catfish in the cold-weather months.

As noted earlier, however, low oxygen levels in some ponds may prevent cats from using these deep-water haunts. In this case, you'll find the fish cruising the shallows. Look for them around points, along weed-lines, in pockets along the shoreline and in any shaded areas along the bank.

Inflowing water attracts cats in any type of pond. Muddy runoff ignites feeding activity, because the inflow carries insects, earthworms and other catfish foods. Cats may also hold in the current near the outflow.

Another sure bet for small-pond catfish is a rocky area. A riprap bank or a natural rock wall, for example, will invariably attract cats.

Common Types of Man-Made Ponds

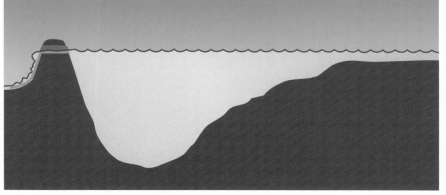

Dammed Ponds. *Created by building an earthen dam across a small stream, a pond of this type usually is deepest at the base of the dam. In some cases, there is a deep trench at the base of the dam where fill was removed to build the structure. Because of the moving water, ponds of this type seldom stratify into temperature layers.*

Bulldozed Ponds. *These ponds are usually round or rectangular, with a bowl-shaped basin. The deepest water is in the center. They are fed by runoff rather than a permanent flow, so there is little mixing; and the water stratifies into temperature layers in summer. The deepest water may not have enough oxygen to support catfish.*

POND-FISHING TECHNIQUES

Fishing catfish in a pond is not much different than fishing them in a lake, but there are a few tricks that can improve your results.

For example, catfish in most ponds feed primarily on sunfish and minnows rather than big-water forage like shad and skipjack herring.

Consequently, live sunfish and minnows (or cut bait made from them) are often the best choice.

Catfish in ponds, especially those that stratify, may feed in surprisingly shallow water. Dangling your bait beneath a float set only a few feet deep will often catch more cats than fishing the bait on the bottom.

Ponds usually hold more cats on a per-acre basis than do larger lakes. Competition for food is often intense, meaning that cats are willing to take baits that they might pay little attention to in bigger waters.

Some savvy anglers have discovered that bass lures, particularly rattling, lipless crankbaits, will cause a competitive reaction among pond-dwelling catfish. It's not unusual to see several cats fighting to get at the bait.

Pond fishing is a relaxing—yet highly effective—catfishing method.

One big advantage to using artificials: you can cover a lot of water in a hurry, making it possible to scout a small pond in a fraction of the time it would take with natural bait.

Because most pond fishermen are shorebound, they can't possibly reach fish more than a long cast from the bank. To improve your odds and draw the fish to you, try chumming. Just toss out some minced fish or meat; or put some chum (p. 133) along with a rock in a burlap or cheesecloth bag tied to a rope, and toss it into the water.

It's not hard to understand why pond fishing for catfish has become so popular. While the bigwater catmen are battling wind and whitecaps, you're relaxing in a lawnchair with a cold drink, watching the world go by— and hauling in cats.

Where to Find Catfish in a Dammed Pond

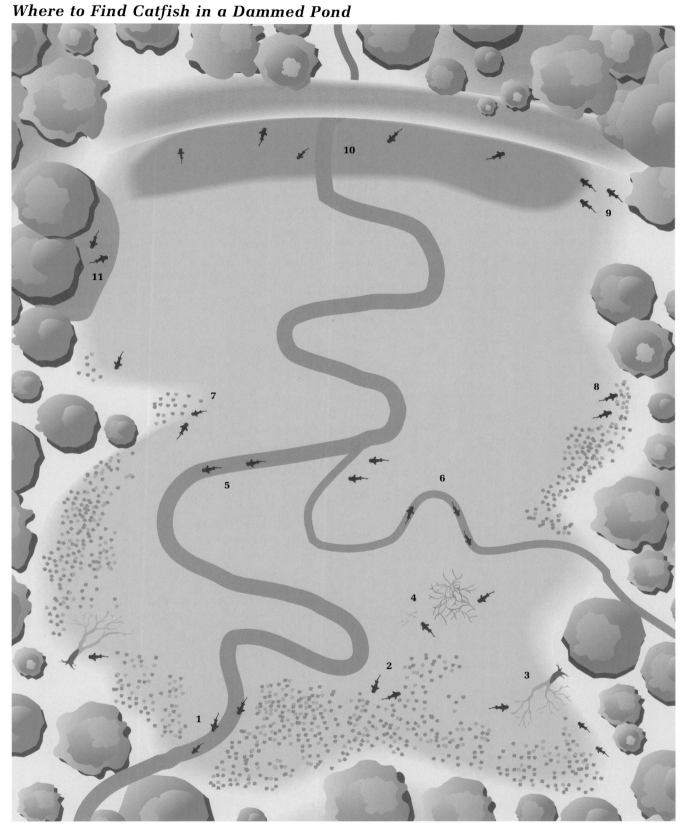

Look for catfish (1) near major inflows, (2) along weedlines, around (3) fallen trees and (4) brush piles, in (5) creek channels and (6) feeder channels, (7) on points, (8) in pockets, (9) in corners of the pond, (10) in the deep slot at the dam's base and (11) in shady areas.

Pond-Fishing Tips

If access to the shoreline of a pond is limited, try chumming to bring the catfish to you. Competition for food is keen in most ponds, so the cats should come freely to the handouts ... and your bait.

A rattling, lipless crankbait emits sound and vibrations that attract catfish. Although a high-speed retrieve will sometimes draw strikes, you'll normally catch more cats with a fairly slow retrieve, letting the bait bump along the bottom.

Bring along a light spinning outfit and some worms to catch the sunfish you need for bait. Keep them in a flow-through minnow bucket.

When fishing in the heat of summer, use an electric thermometer to determine the location of the thermocline. Do not fish in the coldwater zone below the thermocline because the oxygen level is probably too low for catfish.

When bank-fishing on a pond, set your rod in a rod holder that pushes into the ground. Engage the clicker on your baitcasting reel. When you get a bite, you'll hear the clicking sound.

Float Fishing for Cats

Float fishing works well in stratified ponds and lakes, and also in small rivers. In lakes and ponds, float fishing is the best way to keep your bait at the level where cats are suspending because of an oxygen shortage in the depths. If you don't have a temperature gauge to find the thermocline, you'll just have to experiment. In many ponds, the thermocline is surprisingly shallow, only 10 to 15 feet down.

To find the right depth, start by setting your float so your bait is at approximately half the pond's depth. If there's no action at that depth, raise the bait 12 to 18 inches at a time until you start getting bites.

In stream fishing, a float not only signals bites, it allows your bait to drift naturally along the bottom. When the rig comes to an eddy, the float follows the current, making a circular path through the fish-holding zone. Without a float, it would be difficult to find the right amount of weight necessary to keep the rig drifting.

Any kind of float, bobber or cork will do the job when fishing close

A float keeps your bait at the precise depth where cats are suspending.

to shore. But when you're making long casts or fishing in rough water, you'll have better results with an 8- to 12-inch cylindrical float; it provides extra weight for casting and is easy to see at a distance. Even though these floats traditionally are made of balsa wood, plastic versions are more durable and can be rigged in many different ways. Some can even be illuminated with Cyalume light sticks, making them an excellent choice for night fishing.

Float-Fishing Tips

"Color-code" your lines to help keep track of them at night by rigging your floats with different-colored light sticks.

Let the current move your float-fishing rig in a circular pattern to thoroughly cover an eddy. Without a float, your bait would stay in the same place.

CUMBERLAND'S COLOSSAL CATS

by Jeff Samsel

"If you're fishing here, you had better be prepared to hang into a big one," says Donny Hall, a full-time guide on Tennessee's Cumberland River. "You may catch a lot of small catfish, but if you hook into a giant and you're not prepared, you're going to lose him."

Hall and his clients have had their lines—and their hearts—broken on more than one occasion, even when they were fully prepared and doing absolutely nothing wrong.

A few years back, Hall hooked a cat that he simply couldn't handle. It just swam around for awhile, stubbornly refusing to give ground. Eventually, his 80-pound line parted.

Hall, who is not prone to telling "fish stories," is firmly convinced that he had the state-record flathead catfish on his line that winter day.

The Cumberland River rises from a network of rugged creeks atop the Cumberland Plateau in Tennessee and Kentucky, with its main branch forming within Kentucky's borders. From there, the river dips back into Tennessee for most of its length before flowing back into Kentucky and eventually emptying into the Ohio River.

Along the way, the river pauses in the impounded waters behind Cumberland, Cordell Hull, Old Hickory, Cheatham and Barkley dams. Toward the lower end of Barkley, the Cumberland is joined by the Tennessee River, known nationally for its record-caliber catfish.

A large river suitable for barge traffic, the Cumberland is home to channel, flathead and blue catfish. And all three grow to remarkable size in its fertile waters. Cumberland cats enjoy a smorgasbord of aquatic delicacies including crayfish, threadfin and gizzard shad, skipjack herring and various species of sunfish.

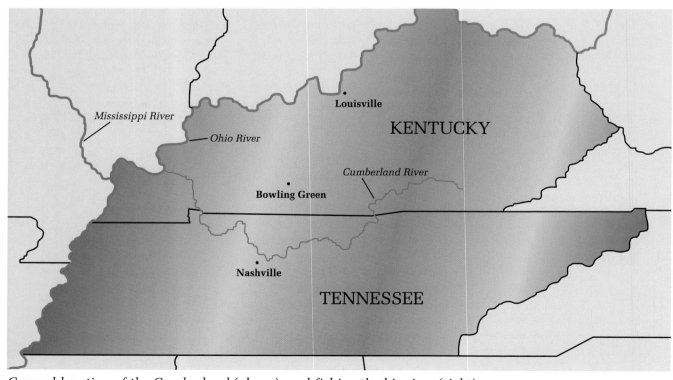

General location of the Cumberland (above), and fishing the big river (right).

Old Hickory Lake.

WHERE AND WHEN

According to Donny Hall, who operates Old Hickory Guide Service, the best catfishing on the Cumberland River begins at Cordell Hull Dam, which forms Old Hickory Lake. Hall works about 160 miles of the river, including both Old Hickory and Cheatham lakes.

Hall, who grew up on the banks of the Cumberland, fishes cats throughout the year. He focuses primarily on medium-sized channels and blues in the warm months, and trophy blues and flatheads in fall and winter.

By far the best time to catch a giant catfish in these waters is late fall through early winter, Hall contends. That's because the big fish are concentrated in certain deep holes scattered along the river.

Hall fishes a very large area of the river, so determining the best spot on a given day is not always easy. Recent catches and patterns that produced in previous seasons are always factors in the decision, but day-to-day conditions have an even larger impact.

As in all river systems, catfish location is influenced by water conditions (level, temperature, color and clarity), wind speed and direction, power generation cycles and baitfish movement patterns.

The two lakes Hall fishes most often are vastly different in character, which often helps in making locational decisions. Old Hickory, known simply as "the lake" by most Nashville anglers, has a wide expanse of open water in the lower half and plenty of broad, shallow coves. Cheatham, or "the river," is riverine from dam to dam and typically has a significant flow.

Old Hickory's water level is held fairly stable, despite the high amount of rainfall the area gets. Cheatham, on the other hand, is a flood-control reservoir, so it fluctuates dramatically according to water-release needs by the U.S. Army Corps of Engineers.

As a general rule, Hall fishes Old Hickory's shallow flats through the spring, moves to deeper holes in both lakes as the weather warms, keys on his best big-fish holes in Cheatham through fall and early winter and then returns to Old Hickory in late winter

Cheatham Lake.

and early spring, when Cheatham is running high and muddy.

Hall has found that the catfish move shallow about the same time crappie do each spring. In fact, when he starts catching a few cats in shallow brush piles while crappie fishing, he knows that it's time to start looking for cats on points at the mouths of coves and on shallow flats with discolored water.

Spring rains usually mean fast shallow-water action. "When the creeks run high, shad move shallow to feed, and the catfish follow them in," Hall explains. After a good rain, even a small creek can muddy up the back of a slough enough to draw in the baitfish.

Whatever the season, Hall has certain spots that have produced in years past and, when conditions are right, he will return to them. "When you find a good place, remember it and go back. Those catfish will probably be there year after year," he says.

The largest concentration of trophy catfish in the Cumberland River lies downstream from where Hall spends most of his time. Countless 50-pound-plus blues are caught each year in the 40-mile reach below the Cheatham Dam. Because this stretch is actually the upper end of Lake Barkley, Tennessee River cats have direct access to these waters. They're drawn by tremendous concentrations of shad and herring that congregate around the Cumberland City Steam Plant.

Hall doesn't fish these big-cat waters as often as he'd like, however, because they're too far from his home. But he recommends them highly. "Go there," he says, "and you can plan on getting your string stretched."

CATFISHING TECHNIQUES

In spring, Hall typically anchors in about 20 feet of water directly over a point at the mouth of a cove. He then spreads lines, using slip-sinker rigs, up on the point and along its sides, usually in 5 to 10 feet of water. Hall's favorite springtime baits include shrimp, chicken livers and cut bait, especially skipjack herring.

If there's brush within casting range and the wind direction allows, Hall may flip out a float rig baited with a small minnow. He knows this technique is effective because of the number of cats he catches while crappie fishing.

Most of the catfish Hall catches in shallow water run from 4 to 10 pounds, but he occasionally takes channels up to 20, along with the odd big blue or flathead. Knowing big fish are always possible, he uses medium-heavy baitcasting rods and Ambassadeur 5500 reels spooled with 50-pound-test Spiderwire.

As summer conditions push the cats deeper, Hall upsizes his gear—partly to contend with the extra depth and

Finding Cumberland Cats

Look for cats on the upstream slope of a deep hole. This is a prime feeding area, because fish lying on the upstream lip have the first chance to grab food carried in by the current.

Cheatham's current, but mostly because of the increased odds of tangling with bigger fish. The Ambassadeur 5500s and medium-heavy rods are replaced with 7000s spooled with 130-pound Spiderwire and heavy custom-made rods constructed from saltwater blanks.

Hall typically uses a single anchor to position his boat upstream of a productive hole, taking current and wind into consideration. He then spreads lines to work different parts of the structure, with some baits down in the hole and others on the slope or even up on the shelf. If he has cover directly below him and is anchored in more than 15 feet of water, Hall might also fish a line or two directly beneath the boat.

During dog days, Hall catches a lot of 30-pound-plus blues, particularly in the upper end of Cheatham, within 10 miles or so of the Old

Hickory Dam. The river below the dam has a tremendous amount of rubble, which the blues use for spawning. "After they spawn, the big females come out and they get kind of ornery," Hall laughs.

Hall's best summer catfish holes offer a combination of structural features, like a major hump close to a deep hole in the old river channel. Washout holes along deep outside bends almost always hold cats, with fish often holding along the upstream slope of the hole.

For dog-day cats, Hall becomes a night stalker. Catfish, especially flatheads, are largely nocturnal feeders and become even more so after hot, bright summer days. The air temperature is much more comfortable, you usually have the river to yourself and the night-bite can be fantastic.

As the heat of summer subsides, Hall begins to get seri-

ous about big cats. For bait, he relies almost exclusively on big chunks of cut skipjack, stringing the weighty offerings on 5/0 to 10/0 hooks and using slip-sinker rigs with as much as 5 ounces of lead to get the bait down in heavy current.

Unlike most trophy catfish specialists, Hall doesn't use live baitfish for flatheads. He has tried a variety of different live bait, but has always caught more big flatheads on cut skipjack.

Donny Hall doesn't mind sharing the wisdom he has gained through a lifetime of fishing the Cumberland River. "I am in the business of teaching people how to catch fish," he says. "I work 160 miles of river, and there's no way I can fish all that. I enjoy seeing other people catch fish." His strategies and techniques can help you catch more cats wherever you fish, too.

Donny Hall with a fat Cumberland blue.

How to Catch Cumberland Cats

Make a slip-sinker rig for use with cut bait by threading on a 1- to 5-ounce egg sinker, adding a large barrel swivel and then tying on a heavy leader. Use a size 1/0 to 3/0 hook for small bait chunks (top); a 5/0 to 10/0 for large baits (bottom).

Big chunks of cut skipjack are Hall's bread-and-butter bait for Cumberland cats, even flatheads.

TIDEWATER BLUES

by Jeff Samsel

Giant catfish addicts know that tidewater rivers produce some of the country's biggest blues. South Carolina's Cooper River, for example, has yielded blues topping the 100-pound mark. Virginia's tidewater rivers, including the James and Rappahannock, receive considerably less press, but both of them produce impressive numbers of trophy blues.

Virginia's state-record blue catfish, weighing 66 pounds, 8 ounces, came from the mouth of the Appomattox River, a James River tributary. But the record has shifted between the two river systems many times since blues were first stocked in the early 1970s.

The James, vast and powerful, drains a fairly flat and highly developed landscape. The narrower Rappahannock winds through undeveloped woodlands, and bluff-shrouded river bends combine with fallen trees to create classic catfish holes. The James has over 50 miles of prime catfish water, as opposed to less than 20 miles for the Rappahannock.

"The James and the Rappahannock are different in a lot of ways, but when it comes to producing big catfish, they rank about the same," says Archie Gold, who regularly fishes Virginia Catfish Association tournaments with his wife, Debra. One year, the couple landed 60 catfish that weighed more than 30 pounds each, 16 of which broke the 40-pound mark. Those catches were fairly well distributed between the two rivers.

"The cats are getting bigger in both rivers," Archie notes. "Twenty-pound fish used to be something special, but now they are common." In 1996, Archie caught a 53½-pound blue, the largest one taken in Virginia that year. Debra was not far behind with the 51-pounder she caught in 1997. "We are all expecting another state record soon," says Archie.

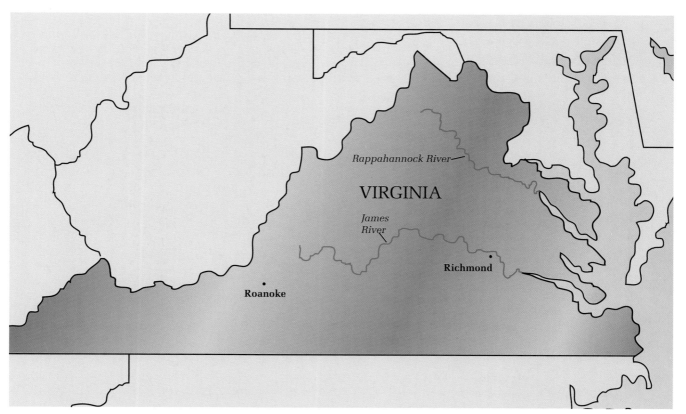

Virginia's premier catfish rivers, the James and the Rappahannock, and landing a tidewater blue (left).

UNDERSTANDING TIDEWATER RIVERS

Tidewater rivers differ from other rivers in that water conditions are constantly changing, mainly because of the moon's gravitational pull on the surface of the earth. The water level in a tidal river fluctuates several feet each day, the river's flow changes direction every 6½ hours and the strength of the current varies enormously depending on moon phase, distance from the river's mouth and amount of runoff.

During an early spring period of high flow and a full moon, for example, the river will practically lie still on an incoming tide. But on an out-

Lower reaches of the James River.

going tide, the current will be so swift that fishing is next to impossible.

With the same moon phase in midsummer, however, an incoming tide will create an upstream current nearly as strong as the current during an outgoing tide.

On many tidal rivers, the best catfishing extends upstream only as far as the fall line. Above that point, the river is not influenced by the tides. Richmond marks the upstream limit of prime catfish water on the James; Fredericksburg, on the Rappahannock.

Best Times

Catfishing is a year-round sport on the James and Rappahannock. Fishing turns tough in late spring, when the blues are spawning, and winter offers a slower bite than other seasons, but big catfish can be caught throughout the year.

According to local catfishing expert Bruce Meyer, blue cats go on a feeding spree in

early spring, as huge schools of blueback herring and shad run upstream from Chesapeake Bay to spawn. Summer and fall yield plenty of big fish too. "We get a lot of three-fish limits of 110 pounds or more on July and August nights," Meyer says, "but late fall probably produces the fastest bite. You get

Tides		
Windmill Point, James River		
JULY 5–11 (EDT)		
	HIGH	LOW
July 5	6:31 a.m.	12:43 a.m.
Sun.	7:01 p.m.	12:33 p.m.
July 6	7:22 a.m.	1:33 a.m.
Mon.	7:47 p.m.	1:21 p.m.
July 7	8:10 a.m.	2:19 a.m.
Tues.	8:31 p.m.	2:07 p.m.
July 8	8:56 a.m.	3:03 a.m.
Wed.	9:14 p.m.	2:53 p.m.
July 9	9:40 a.m.	3:46 a.m.
Thurs.	9:57 p.m.	3:38 p.m.
July 10	10:25 a.m.	4:28 a.m.
Fri.	10:40 p.m.	4:24 p.m.
July 11	11:09 a.m.	5:10 a.m.
Sat.	11:25 p.m.	5:11 p.m.

Magazines and local newspapers publish tide tables, which show when high and low tides will occur in different spots on tidal rivers.

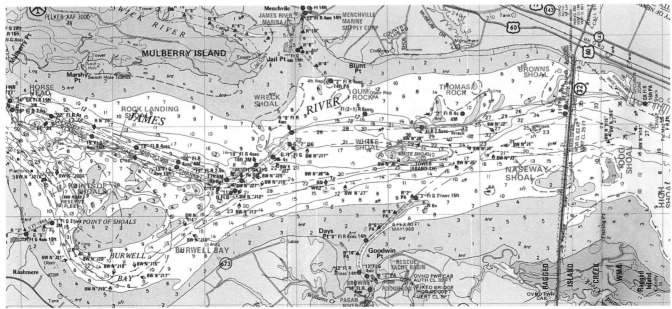

Detailed depth charts are available for the James (above) and the Rappahannock (opposite).

a couple of cold days and those catfish will eat and eat, preparing for tougher times ahead."

Meyer doesn't care which way the water is flowing, as long as it is pushing hard. "Channel catfish hit well on the slack tide," he notes, "but blues seem to like the water moving. I do best during the first and last hour and a half of each tide cycle."

Savvy tidewater anglers pay close attention to tide tables, which appear daily in local newspapers, to plan their catfish outings.

Tidewater rivers are big, and different in that you have to work with the tides to find big cats.

Best Places

Meyer's favorite spots on the James include various channels used for ship navigation, and holes that have formed around sunken barges. Currents ripping around those barges through thousands of tide cycles have scoured holes that are 25 or more feet deep and make prime holding areas for big blue catfish.

On the Rappahannock, Meyer primarily fishes bluff holes. "The deepest hole that is the closest to the bank is the one I like best," he explains. Cliffs that rise on outside bends typically reveal such holes. Timber in the bottom of a hole also adds a lot of appeal for catfish.

On either river, the Golds seek out the deepest water they can find, which is commonly 40 or more feet deep. On the James, they look for humps within long, deep stretches. "The humps break the current," Archie explains, "and the big cats lay around them, waiting for dinner to wash through."

Holes on the Rappahannock are more clearly defined than those on the James. Within the holes, Archie looks for big trees to key on. "The Rappahannock is loaded with woodwork," he points out.

But the good holes in tidal rivers are constantly changing. "The holes don't even stay in the same places," Meyer says. "A spot that produced a bunch of catfish one summer may be filled in the next year—but somewhere nearby a new one will form that will be just as good. It's just a matter of finding it."

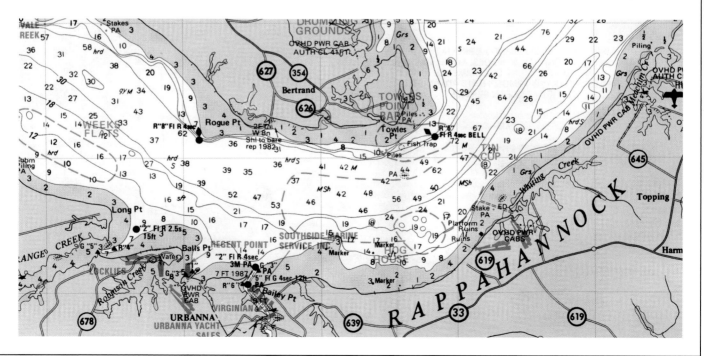

Meyer with a nice Rappahannock blue.

TIDEWATER TACTICS

Bruce Meyer and the Golds use similar techniques for catching big blues in tidal rivers, but there are some subtle differences.

Meyer's Technique

Meyer positions his boat on the upstream side of a hole, taking both current and wind direction into account when he sets his anchors. He fishes all his lines out the back of the boat, varying the lengths and angles of his casts to put some baits in the deepest part of the hole, some on the slope and others on the lip, above the drop.

Meyer typically uses slip-sinker rigs with size 1/0 to 5/0 wide-bend hooks baited with cut gizzard shad. He sometimes substitutes flattened slip-sinkers for the traditional egg sinkers, which

tend to roll down the slope. The sinker must be heavy enough to hold the bait in place, even in strong current.

The shad, which are typically a foot long, are normally filleted with the skin and scales left intact. The fillets, entrails and head are all used as bait. "We pretty much use everything but the ribs and the backbone," says Meyer. A 7-inch fillet might be used whole, or it might be cut into strips.

To handle cats that could top the 50-pound mark, Meyer relies on medium-heavy-power flippin' sticks and Ambassadeur 6500C reels spooled with 25-pound-test Stren Super-Tough mono.

The Golds' Method

Archie and Debra normally anchor just upstream of the highest part of a hump or the

thickest cover within a hole. They fan their lines all the way around the boat to thoroughly cover the hole, using enough weight to hold bottom, even with lines cast upstream of their boat position. They also fish a few lines directly below the boat, reeling up a few cranks to keep the bait off the bottom.

For fishing cut bait, the Golds use a 3-way rig. For live bait, including bream, eels or perch, they use a slip-sinker rig with a flattened sinker, much like the rig Meyer prefers (right).

Archie prefers baitcasting tackle, pairing Penn 320 GTL reels with Berkley catfish series rods. Debra normally uses saltwater spinning gear. Both spool up with 30-pound-test Ande monofilament.

Most fishermen consider the Rappahannock a tougher river to fish, and its cats seem to be more fickle than those in the James. "One day you'll really catch them, and another day they won't cooperate at all," says Archie, "even with conditions pretty much the same. That doesn't happen on the James."

The difference, Archie believes, may lie in the abundance of forage. There are always plenty of shad around on the James, so the fish don't have to travel far to find food. Consequently, you know right where to find them. But forage is considerably scarcer on the Rappahannock, meaning the fish are much less predictable.

Anglers fishing tidal rivers must contend with a lot more variables than those who fish inland streams. As tidewater anglers often say: the only real constant is change. But the giant cats these rivers produce more than make up for the inconvenience.

Both Meyer and the Golds rely on a slip-sinker rig with a flattened weight for fishing live bait. This type of weight works well in current, because it won't roll.

For fishing cut bait, the Golds use a 3-way rig with a dropper line and bell sinker (2 to 8 ounces) at the bottom and a size 7/0 to 9/0 Owner live-bait hook tied to an 18-inch leader.

How to Fillet a Gizzard Shad

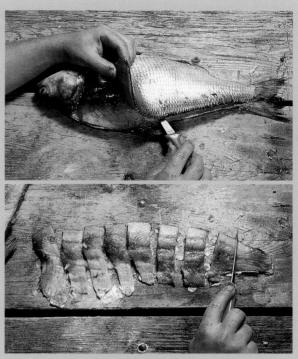

Using a sharp fillet knife, make a cut behind the gill down to the backbone, then turn the blade and run it along the backbone toward the tail to remove the fillet (top). Run the blade behind the rib bones to remove them. Repeat the procedure on the other side. For large cats, use the whole fillet; for smaller ones, cut it in strips (bottom).

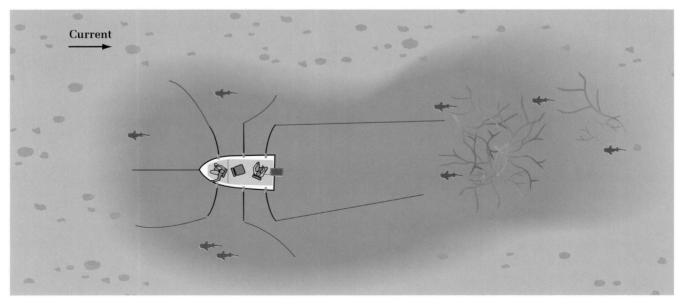

The Golds often anchor in a hole just upstream of a brush pile or hump, spreading lines all around the boat. One or two lines are generally fished directly beneath the boat with baits reeled up a foot or two off the bottom.

CHUMMIN' UP TO CATS

by Jeff Samsel

Anglers have long understood the importance of appealing to a catfish's sense of smell. Blood baits, cut baits, shrimp, chicken livers and all kinds of stinkbaits, whether commercially manufactured or home-brewed, draw cats in by their noses. Only a smattering of catfishermen, however, have taken the fish-attracting concept a giant step farther by adding the technique of chumming to their arsenal.

Chumming, which has always been popular in saltwater-fishing circles, simply means putting out an attractant with a scent that is strong enough to draw the fish to you, greatly shortening the time between bites.

TYPES OF CHUM

Catfishermen have tried chumming with just about every smelly substance imaginable. And they have tried every possible method to keep their chum in place so it draws fish to the desired spot. The chum needs to break up or spread so it gives off a strong scent, yet the material must stay in place. Otherwise, the fish won't home in on the spot you're fishing.

Commonly used types of chum include minced baitfish, coagulated blood, chicken entrails and other parts, fermented grain, dog food, cheese scraps and a variety of commercial concoctions.

One big consideration in selecting chum is the rate at which it dissolves.

Chum that dissolves quickly emits a more intense scent but for a shorter period of time, so it is a good choice for a short outing. Blood and ground-up fish, for example, have a very strong odor, but their appeal tends to be short lived. They are good choices when you're not able to "pre-chum" an area.

Slow-release chum (such as dog food, fermented grain and commercial chum blocks) may not concentrate catfish quite as much but tends to set up a "food chain" that attracts baitfish, crayfish and other forage which, in turn, draws cats and keeps them around.

Popular Types of Chum

Popular types of chum include (1) prepared chum blocks, (2) coagulated blood, (3) chum pellets, (4) fermented grain, (5) dog food and (6) chum sticks.

WHERE TO CHUM

Experienced chummers look for the structural features that typically draw cats. But beyond that, they also take into account the direction and approximate length of the chum line (the scent zone resulting from the chum). Wind may play a minor role in distributing the scent, but current is much more important. Even in lakes, there is usually some water movement.

In a river, chumming is most effective in a long reach that has plenty of good catfish cover. This way, the chum can dissipate over a large area that holds fish.

In large lakes, the current may not be apparent but, if you watch closely, you might be able to see some water movement. One of the best ways to detect the movement is to toss out a line with a float attached. If you see the float moving against the wind or at an angle to it, you know there's some current. Then you can plan the placement of your chum accordingly. Be sure that it drifts into spots likely to hold cats.

Chumming may not be as effective in small lakes that have no significant current, because it takes so long for the scent to spread. But it will spread eventually, and the scent will move out in all directions.

If possible, spread your chum near good cover, like a logjam or big sunken brush pile. This will help keep the cats around after they have moved in to check out the chum.

CHUMMING TECHNIQUES

In addition to knowing where to chum, you must also know when. If you spread your chum too much in advance of your outing, it will be dissipated by the time you start fishing. But if you don't get it out soon enough, the cats may not have enough time to react to it. Your tim-

Good Spots for Chumming

A point at the mouth of a cove is a perfect place to chum in still water, because the scent can spread into the cove as well as the main lake.

In a reservoir, try chumming at the confluence of the main river channel and a creek channel. This way, the scent can spread down both channels, increasing your odds of drawing catfish.

ing depends mainly on the type of chum you're using and the type of water you're fishing.

In a river, where the chum spreads rapidly, most anglers do their chumming only an hour or two in advance, especially if they're using chum that breaks up or dissolves rapidly. On the other hand, fishermen using slow-release commercial chum in a lake setting often start chumming a day or two before they plan on fishing.

Commercial trotliners have long understood the value of chumming the same areas for extended periods of time. They select an area with good cover and keep it well-chummed for several weeks. This way, they can harvest large numbers of cats without having to move their lines.

To keep the bulk of their chum together but allow dissolved particles to escape, catfishermen often place their chum in a mesh or burlap bag or a covered 5-gallon bucket with plenty of holes drilled in it. The bag or bucket is then tied to a rope and lowered to the bottom. Depending on the density of the chum, a few ounces of lead may be needed to sink the contraption.

It's important to mark the precise spot where you place the chum so you can come back later and anchor up in the proper location. Many anglers like to chum an area next to a flooded tree or stick-up; this way they know right where to fish. If there is nothing to mark the spot, toss out a marker buoy or find a good landmark.

Laws concerning chumming vary considerably from state to state. In some states, it is not permitted. Be sure to check your local regulations.

Chumming takes a little extra time and makes for some extra work, but once you witness the results, you won't mind a bit.

Where access is limited, shore fishermen can draw catfish to a spot that wouldn't otherwise hold many fish by chumming it a few hours before they plan to fish it.

In a river, spread your chum just upstream of a brush pile or logjam near the upper end of a long hole. The cover encourages cats that are drawn to the chum to stay in the area.

Chumming with Fermented Grain

2 *Pour at least a gallon of fermented grain in each spot you will be fishing on a particular day. Mark the spot with a marker buoy.*

3 *Wait an hour or two, then drop anchor just upwind of the buoy so your boat is directly over the spot you chummed.*

1 *Fill a 5-gallon pail about two-thirds full of wheat or cracked corn. Add a cup of sugar and enough water to cover the grain by 2 or 3 inches. Put a lid on the pail and allow the grain to soak up the water; this should take about 2 days. Then add enough water to cover the grain again, and replace the lid. It will take about 5 days before the grain ferments and the chum is ready to use. If you plan on doing a lot of chumming, prepare several pails of grain at the same time.*

4 *Pinch a ½- to 1-ounce sinker onto your line about a foot above a size 1/0 hook, then add a chunk of cut bait or mold on some stinkbait or cheesebait, making sure the point is covered.*

Get a 5-gallon bucket of cow blood at a slaughter house and keep it in a cool spot for several days until it congeals. Then drill holes in the bucket and lower it to the bottom on a rope. Cats will follow the blood trail to your boat.

Attach a rope to a commercially made chum block and lower it to the bottom. You can also tie it off to a bridge or tree limb. Some blocks last for 6 to 8 days.

Place your chum in a burlap bag, add a few rocks for weight and tie a rope around the neck of the bag to seal it. The bag holds the chum material in place, yet the scent can easily dissipate.

Toss out one or more Chum-Stiks when you arrive at your spot. They dissolve quickly and start drawing cats right away.

CLEANING & COOKING CATFISH

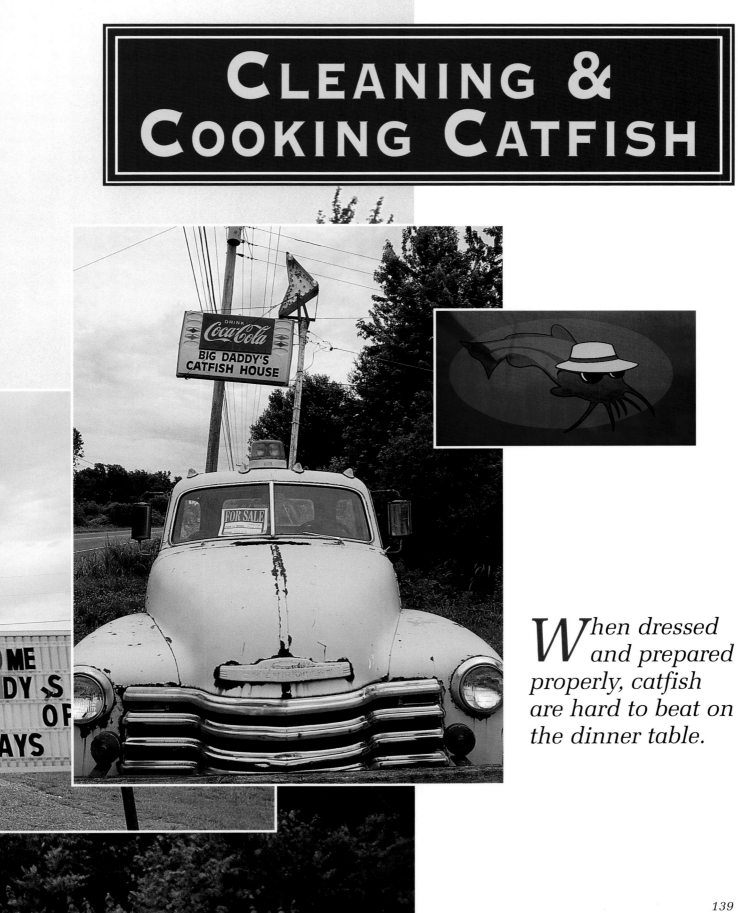

When dressed and prepared properly, catfish are hard to beat on the dinner table.

CLEANING & COOKING METHODS

Catfish are one of the finest tasting fish that swim in fresh water. Their flesh is firm, moist, flaky and offers a mild flavor with very little "fishy" taste.

When compared to beef, chicken or pork, catfish is low in total fat, saturated fat and cholesterol. It is also high in protein and provides Omega-3 fatty acids, which researchers have found to reduce the risk of heart disease.

CLEANING TECHNIQUES

For the best possible flavor, you must care for your catfish properly. Ideally, they should be killed, gutted and placed on ice immediately after they are caught. Fish kept on a stringer or in a warm livewell all day will simply not taste as good.

Bullheads and small catfish are usually pan-dressed (p. 142). Medium- to large-sized catfish are normally filleted or steaked (p. 143).

PAN DRESSING

This method gives you a solid piece of fish flesh that can be pan-fried or baked. None of the flesh goes to waste, and the bones can be removed at the dinner table. You can pan-dress the fish on a cleaning board, but many fishermen prefer to hang the fish on a hook to make skinning easier.

FILLETING

Fillets cook faster and more thoroughly than do pan-

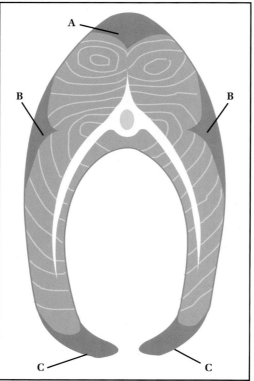

Most of the fatty tissue (and contaminants) are located (a) along the fish's back, (b) along the sides and (c) along the belly. This fatty flesh is usually reddish or darker in color, so it is easy to see and remove.

dressed catfish, and most people think they taste better, as well. There are two basic filleting methods: cut off the fillets and then remove the skin with your knife or remove the skin first and then slice off the fillets.

STEAKING

Steaking is mainly an option for medium-sized catfish. Large catfish are hard to steak because it's so difficult to cut through the backbone. The technique is simple: just skin the fish, remove the entrails and then slice off steaks that are about 1 inch thick.

REDUCING FAT & CONTAMINANTS

Catfish taken from big rivers and even from some smaller rivers and lakes may contain contaminants. These substances are found mainly in the fatty tissue. It's a good idea to remove as much of this tissue as possible, not only to reduce the fat and contaminant level, but also to improve the taste. Another reason to remove the fat: the fish can be frozen for a longer periods of time without turning rancid.

Cleaning & Cooking Catfish   141

1 With a sharp fillet knife, cut through the skin on both sides of the body just behind the head, and along the backbone to a point just behind the dorsal spine.

2 Using a skinning pliers, grasp the skin, pull it back to the tail and remove it. Do the same on the opposite side of the fish.

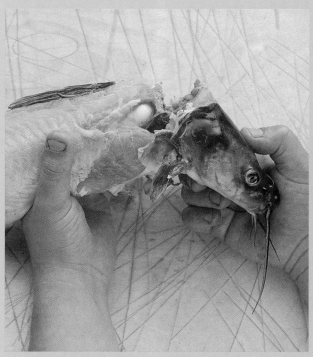

3 Remove the head by bending it downward until the backbone snaps. Continue pulling to remove the entrails.

4 Pull the remaining fins out with a pliers. On larger fish, you may first have to cut along both sides of the fins with a knife before pulling.

Steaking Catfish

1 Using a sharp butcher knife, cut the skinned carcass into inch-thick steaks. Trim the fatty tissue from the back, sides and belly.

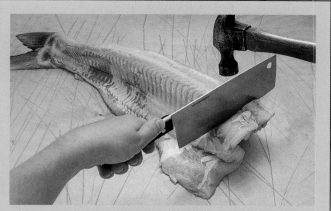

2 If necessary, use a meat cleaver and a hammer to sever the backbone of a large catfish.

Filleting Catfish

1 Make an angled cut from just behind the head down to the fish's midline. Then turn the blade and continue cutting to the vent. Be careful not to puncture the intestines.

2 Hold the fish's head and work your knife along the backbone all the way to the tail to remove the fillet. Repeat the procedure on the opposite side.

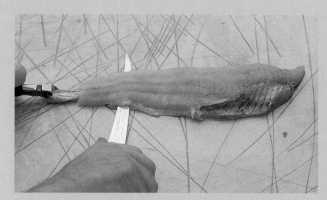

3 Hold the tail with skinning pliers and then skin the fillets by angling your knife blade down and using a sawing motion while pulling on the skin with your other hand.

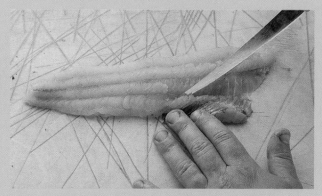

4 Remove the rib bones and elipleural bones (connecting anchor bones set at a right angle to the rib cage) and trim off any fatty tissue on the back, sides and belly.

RECIPES

Ask a group of well-travelled anglers to name their favorite table fish, and catfish would surely come up high on the list. Although catfish are traditionally prepared by frying, anglers are discovering many low-fat preparation methods that are equally tasty.

So here are our all-time favorite catfish recipes, from NAFC members as well as renowned fish-and-game chefs. Enjoy!

Skillet-Fried Catfish Nuggets

1 cup milk
1 egg
1 package saltine crackers, crushed very fine*
1 tsp. seasoning salt (or to taste)
2 lbs. catfish fillets, cut into 2-inch chunks
Vegetable oil for pan-frying

Blend milk and egg in small bowl; mix crushed saltines and seasoning salt in wide bowl. Dip fish nuggets into milk mixture, then roll in cracker mixture. Heat $^1/_2$ inch oil in cast-iron skillet over medium-high heat; fry nuggets, a few at a time, until golden brown on all sides. Drain on paper towels. (This recipe is also delicious with bass, walleye or crappie.)

*Tip: Put crackers in plastic bag and crush with a rolling pin, rolling toward the open end (this lets the air out of the bag). Add seasoning salt and shake. Place dipped fish nuggets into bag and shake to coat.

8 to 10 appetizer servings.

Hush Puppies

$1^1/_2$ cups cornmeal
$^1/_2$ cup all-purpose flour
$^1/_3$ cup sugar
2 tsp. baking powder
1 tsp. salt
1 small onion, finely chopped
1 egg, beaten
$^3/_4$ cup milk
Vegetable oil for deep-frying

Sift cornmeal, flour, sugar, baking powder and salt into bowl. Add onion. Blend in egg and milk, stirring just until lumps disappear. Drop by teaspoons, a few at a time, into hot deep fryer. Fry until golden brown. Drain on paper towels.

8 to 10 servings.

Catfish and Scallops with Mushrooms

1 cup milk
1 egg
2 to 4 catfish fillets
1 cup cornmeal
$^1/_4$ cup vegetable oil
$^1/_4$ lb. scallops
4 oz. sliced mushrooms
$^1/_2$ tsp. crumbled dried basil
1 cup room-temperature beer

Blend milk and egg in small bowl. Dip catfish fillets into milk mixture, then roll in cornmeal. Heat oil in large skillet over medium-high heat; fry fillets until cooked through and golden brown on both sides. Transfer fillets to warm platter and keep warm. Add scallops to skillet; cook over medium heat until firm and opaque. Use slotted spoon to place scallops on top of fillets. Add mushrooms, basil, and salt and pepper to taste to skillet; cook until mushrooms are tender. Add beer to skillet; cook over high heat until liquid has almost completely cooked away. Spoon mushrooms on top of fish and scallops.

2 to 4 servings.

Fried Catfish and Hush Puppies.

Catfish Anna

1 medium onion, thinly sliced
1 large zucchini, thinly sliced
1 medium tomato, peeled and thinly sliced
$1/2$ tsp. crumbled dried oregano
1 to $1^1/2$ lbs. catfish fillets
$1/3$ cup white wine or water
1 cup sour cream
$1/2$ tsp. mustard
$1/8$ tsp. salt
Paprika

Heat oven to 350°F. Lightly oil 9 x 13-inch baking dish. Arrange onions on bottom of dish. Top with zucchini slices, then with tomato slices. Sprinkle oregano over; salt and pepper to taste. Top with catfish fillets; add wine. Cover dish with foil and bake until fish flakes when probed with fork, about 25 minutes. Transfer fish and vegetables to warm oven-proof platter. In small bowl, combine sour cream, mustard and $1/8$ teaspoon salt. Spread sour cream mixture over fish; sprinkle with paprika. Broil until topping is browned and bubbly, about 5 minutes.

4 to 6 servings.

Catfish with Creole Sauce

Creole sauce:
$1/2$ cup chopped onion
$1/2$ cup chopped green pepper
$1/2$ cup thinly sliced okra
2 T. margarine
1 16-oz. can tomatoes, cut up, juice reserved
2 T. tomato paste
1 cup tomato juice
$1/2$ tsp. salt
$1^1/2$ tsp. sugar
Ground cayenne pepper to taste

6 catfish fillets
1 tsp. minced garlic
1 tsp. paprika
1 tsp. crumbled dried tarragon

Heat oven to 375°F. To make Creole sauce: In heavy saucepan, cook onion, green pepper and okra in margarine over medium heat, stirring frequently, until onion is tender. Add tomatoes and reserved juice, along with remaining sauce ingredients. Stir well. Heat to boiling; reduce heat and simmer 10 minutes. Season catfish with garlic, paprika and tarragon. Place fillets on lightly oiled cookie sheet. Bake until fish flakes when probed with fork. Serve sauce with catfish.

4 to 6 servings.

Catfish Anna.

Catfishing Strategies

Baked Catfish

1 to 2 lbs. catfish fillets
1/4 cup margarine or butter (1/2 stick)
1/2 cup dry onion-ring mix

Heat oven to 350°F. Rinse catfish; set aside. Place margarine in 9 x 13-inch baking dish; place in oven until margarine melts. Roll damp (but not wet) fillets in onion-ring mix. Arrange coated fish in single layer in baking dish; turn immediately to coat second side of fish with margarine. Bake until fish flakes when probed with fork, 15 to 20 minutes.

2 to 4 servings.

Fishburgers

1 lb. catfish fillets
1 egg, beaten
1/2 cup bread crumbs
2 T. finely chopped fresh parsley
1 onion, finely minced
Hot sauce to taste
4 hamburger buns

Grind catfish with meat grinder or food processor. In mixing bowl, combine ground fish with all other ingredients except hamburger buns; add salt and pepper to taste. Form fish mixture into 4 patties. Place on tray covered with waxed paper; cover and refrigerate at least 1/2 hour. Grill or pan-fry until cooked through. Serve on buns.

4 servings.

Cheesy Catfish, Please!

1/4 cup grated Parmesan cheese
1/4 cup all-purpose flour
1 tsp. paprika
1/2 tsp. pepper
2 lbs. catfish fillets
1/4 cup milk
2 T. margarine, melted
3 oz. shredded mozzarella cheese (about 3/4 cup)
3 oz. shredded cheddar cheese (about 3/4 cup)

Heat oven to 400°F. Combine Parmesan cheese, flour, paprika and pepper in bowl. Dip catfish fillets into milk, then coat with Parmesan mixture. Place fillets in baking dish; drizzle with melted margarine. Bake until fish is golden and flaky, 15 to 20 minutes. Mix shredded cheeses together and sprinkle over fish; broil until bubbly.

6 to 8 servings.

Catfish Burgers.

Micro-Easy Calico Catfish

1 medium white potato, pared and cubed

2 ears corn-on-the-cob, cut into 1-inch pieces

2 medium tomatoes, peeled and quartered

1 medium zucchini, cut into 1-inch pieces

$1/4$ cup chopped onion

$1^1/2$ cups chicken broth

2 T. butter

$1/2$ tsp. crumbled dried basil

$1/2$ tsp. crumbled dried oregano

$1/2$ tsp. salt

$1^1/2$ lbs. cooked catfish, cut into cubes

In deep, microwave-safe 2-quart casserole, combine all ingredients except catfish. Cover and microwave on HIGH until vegetables are barely tender, 10 to 15 minutes, stirring once. Add fish cubes. Cover and microwave on HIGH until fish is thoroughly heated, 3 to 4 minutes.

4 servings.

Blackened Catfish

Seasoning mixture:

1 T. paprika

2 tsp. salt

$1/2$ tsp. freshly ground black pepper

$1/2$ tsp. ground cayenne pepper

1 tsp. onion powder

1 tsp. white pepper

$1/2$ tsp. crumbled dried thyme leaves

$1/2$ tsp. garlic powder

Skinned catfish fillets (the seasoning mixture is sufficient for about 2 pounds fillets)

Melted butter

Be sure your kitchen is very well ventilated before doing this; or cook outdoors on a portable propane stove or charcoal grill.

Mix seasoning mixture in small jar; a spice bottle with shaker lid works well. Heat cast-iron skillet or griddle over high heat for 10 minutes. While skillet heats, pat catfish fillets with paper towel. Brush with melted butter. Sprinkle liberally with seasoning mixture; turn and repeat on second side. When pan has heated sufficiently, add fillets in a single layer. Allow to sear very well on the bottom. Turn and sear the other side; if the fillets are sticking to the pan, they are not ready to turn yet. When properly seared, the fillets will "release" from the skillet. Cook on second side until fish is just cooked through.

Catfish and Oyster Stew

$1/2$ cup all-purpose flour

1 tsp. salt

$1/4$ tsp. white pepper

3 cups catfish cubes (cut fillets into 1-inch cubes before measuring)

2 T. butter

2 T. finely minced shallots (or substitute red onions)

$1/4$ cup sherry wine

2 cups canned oysters with liquid*

$1/2$ tsp. Worcestershire sauce

$1/2$ cup heavy cream

1 tsp. chopped fresh parsley

Fresh cracked black pepper to taste

Mix flour, salt and white pepper in pie plate. Roll catfish cubes in flour mixture and shake off excess. In large pot, heat butter over medium-high heat until melted and bubbling. Add fish; cook about 20 seconds per side. Add shallots, sherry, oysters and liquid, and Worcestershire sauce. Heat just to boiling. Reduce heat and simmer about 2 minutes. Place cream in 1-cup measure. With ladle, remove about $1/4$ cup hot liquid from pot and blend into cream. Pour cream mixture into pot. Cook just until cream is heated through; do not boil. Ladle stew into serving bowls; top each with parsley and black pepper.

6 to 8 servings.

Blackened Catfish.

*Tip: Fresh, shucked oysters can be substituted; add about a cup of canned clam juice with the fresh oysters.

Catfish Stir-Fry

1 T. cornstarch
1 T. soy sauce
2 cups chicken stock
1 tsp. finely minced fresh
    gingerroot
1 1/2 T. vegetable oil

Vegetable mix (all cut into 1/4-inch slices):

1 cup sliced onions
1 cup sliced carrots
1 cup sliced celery
1 cup sliced red pepper
1 cup sliced fresh mushrooms

3 cups catfish strips (cut fillets into pieces the size of your little finger before measuring)
4 cups hot cooked white rice

In medium bowl, blend cornstarch and soy sauce.

Add chicken stock and gingerroot; set aside. Heat oil in wok or heavy-bottomed large skillet over high heat until a haze forms over the oil. Add vegetable mix and cook 4 minutes, stirring and tossing frequently. Add chicken stock mixture; heat to simmering. Add catfish strips and cook, stirring frequently, until fish flakes when probed with fork. Serve over rice.

4 to 6 servings.

Mississippi Grilled Catfish

2 catfish fillets
Juice from 1 lemon (about $1/4$ cup)
1 stick butter or margarine
2 cloves garlic, minced
1 tsp. dry mustard
1 tsp. salt
$1/2$ tsp. pepper

Prepare charcoal grill. Brush catfish with lemon juice; set aside. Combine remaining lemon juice, butter, garlic, mustard, salt and pepper in small pan. Heat over low heat until butter melts and liquid is simmering. When coals are ready, grease grill rack and position 4 inches above coals. Grill fish 6 minutes per side, basting several times; fish should flake easily when probed with fork.

2 servings.

Little PeeDee River Catfish Stew

6 slices fatback salt pork ($1/4$-inch slices)
3 large onions, chopped
5 lbs. catfish fillets
4 cans (16 oz. each) tomatoes, juice reserved
$1/4$ cup soy sauce
1 tsp. paprika
2 T. Tabasco sauce, or to taste
Cornstarch as necessary
Hot cooked rice, or bread or saltine crackers

In 12-quart pot, fry fatback over medium-low heat until crisp. Transfer to bowl; set aside. Add two-thirds of the chopped onions to drippings; cook for about 3 minutes. Add catfish and $2^{1}/2$ cups water; return fatback slices to pot. Simmer until fillets fall apart, stirring occasionally. While fish is simmering, combine tomatoes and juice, soy sauce, paprika, Tabasco and remaining chopped onion in blender;

purée until smooth. Add salt and pepper to taste. Add tomato mixture to cooked fish; heat to gentle boil. Use cornstarch to thicken to desired consistency. Serve over rice, or with a loaf of bread or saltine crackers.

10 to 12 servings.

Catfish Chowder

$1/3$ lb. sliced bacon, cut into $1/4$-inch pieces
$1^{1}/2$ lbs. catfish fillets, cut into 1-inch chunks
3/4 cup coarsely chopped onion
2 medium baking potatoes, peeled and diced (about $1^{1}/4$ pounds)
Saltine crackers (about $1/4$ of a box)
Freshly ground black pepper to taste
2 cups half-and-half or milk

Sprinkle one-third of the bacon over bottom of heavy 6-quart kettle. Top with one-third of the fish chunks. Sprinkle one-third of the onions and one-third of the potatoes over fish. Crush 6 saltines over potatoes. Grind fresh black pepper over crackers. Repeat these layers twice. Add water to not quite cover top layer; there should be about an inch that is not covered. Cook, uncovered, over medium heat until the water is absorbed and bacon on bottom has browned slightly, about one hour; do not stir. Add half-and-half. Heat, uncovered, just until half-and-half is hot; do not boil. Stir well before serving; add salt to taste.

6 to 8 servings.

Deep-Fried Catfish

$1/2$ cup buttermilk
$3/4$ cup yellow cornmeal

Vegetable oil for deep-frying
$1^{1}/2$ to 2 lbs. small whole catfish, heads and skin removed

Heat oven to 175°F. Pour buttermilk into shallow dish; place cornmeal on waxed paper. In deep fryer or heavy, deep saucepan, heat 2 to 3 inches oil to 375°F. Dip catfish into buttermilk, then roll in cornmeal. Fry a few fish at a time until deep golden brown and cooked through, about 4 minutes, turning fish once or twice. Drain fish on paper towels; keep warm in oven while you fry remaining fish.

4 servings.

Catfish Jambalaya Stew

1 to 2 lbs. frozen catfish chunks*
1 large onion, diced ($1/4$-inch dice)
1 qt. cut okra
Diced bell pepper to taste
1 jalapeño pepper, sliced
2 to 3 cups rice
1 or 2 cans (16 oz. each) Italian-style stewed tomatoes
1 can ($10^{3}/4$ oz) condensed cream of mushroom soup
$1/2$ tsp. crumbled dried oregano, and other herbs to taste
Lemon pepper to taste
$1/2$ to 1 lb. shrimp, peeled and deveined (optional)
Jalapeño cornbread

Combine all ingredients except shrimp and cornbread in slow-cooker; add 2 to 3 cups water (depending on the amount of rice used). Cook on low heat 6 to 8 hours, until fish flakes and okra is tender; add shrimp during last hour of cooking. Serve with jalapeño corn bread.

*Tip: If using fresh catfish, cook other ingredients 2 to 3 hours before adding fish. To prepare for this dish, cut catfish fillets into chunks before freezing, and you'll be ready to go when you want to make a batch of this delicious stew. 6 to 8 servings.

Catfish Jambalaya Stew.

Baked Catfish

1/4 cup cornmeal
1/4 cup all-purpose flour
1/4 cup grated Parmesan cheese
1 tsp. paprika
1/2 tsp. salt
1/2 tsp. black pepper
1/2 tsp. ground cayenne pepper
1 egg white

2 T. skim milk
4 catfish fillets (4 oz. each)
1 T. sesame seeds
Butter-flavored cooking spray
Fresh lemon wedges

Heat oven to 350°F. In pie plate, combine cornmeal, flour, Parmesan cheese, paprika, salt and peppers; mix well. Whisk together egg white and milk in mixing bowl. Dip catfish fillets into egg white mixture, then roll in cornmeal mixture. Sprinkle with sesame seeds and spray with cooking spray. Place on baking sheet. Bake until fish flakes when probed

Catfish Casino.

with fork, about 30 minutes. Serve with lemon wedges.

4 servings.

Cajun Catfish

2 cups cornmeal
$1/2$ to 1 cup all-purpose flour
2 T. chili powder blend
2 to 3 T. garlic powder
$1/2$ to 1 tsp. salt
1 to 2 tsp. pepper
$1/2$ to 1 tsp. seasoning of your choice (oregano, parsley, paprika, onion powder)
4 to 6 small catfish fillets
4 egg whites, lightly beaten
Hot cooked seasoned rice

Heat oven to 400°F. Place wire rack on cookie sheet; spray with non-stick spray. Mix dry ingredients in shallow bowl. Dip catfish fillets into egg whites, then roll in dry ingredients. Arrange in single layer on wire rack. Bake until fish flakes when probed with fork, about 10 minutes. Serve with rice.

4 to 6 servings.

Catfish Casino

$1/2$ cup all-purpose flour
1 tsp. salt
$1/4$ tsp. white pepper
4 catfish fillets
2 T. butter
1 T. olive oil
$1/2$ cup diced red bell peppers ($1/4$-inch dice)
$1/2$ cup sliced scallions ($1/4$-inch slices)
$1/2$ cup cooked diced bacon
1 T. drained capers
1 tsp. Worcestershire sauce
1 lemon, cut into 4 wedges

Mix flour, salt and pepper in pie plate. Roll catfish fillets in flour mixture and shake off excess. In large skillet, heat butter over medium heat until melted and bubbling. Add fillets. Cook until golden brown on both sides. While fillets are cooking, heat olive oil in medium skillet over medium heat. Add peppers and scallions; sauté about 1 minute. Add bacon, capers and Worcestershire sauce; stir to combine. Transfer cooked fillets to heated platter. Top with pepper mixture; serve with lemon wedges.

4 servings.

Crunchy Catfish Fingers

4 catfish fillets
$1/4$ cup butter ($1/2$ stick), optional
1 cup cornmeal
1 cup grated Parmesan cheese
1 T. parsley flakes
1 cup all-purpose flour
1 T. salt
1 tsp. white pepper
2 eggs
$3/4$ cup milk
2 cups vegetable oil
2 lemons, cut in half
Seasoning of choice (Cajun, BBQ, lemon pepper or garlic salt)

Heat oven to 175°F. Cut catfish fillets into 5-inch-long pieces; if fillets are thick, slice on bias. Melt butter over low heat or in microwave. Skim off any foam on the surface. Let stand several minutes, then pour clear golden liquid into small bowl, leaving behind and discarding milky white residue. Mix cornmeal, Parmesan cheese and parsley in pie plate. In another pie plate, mix flour, salt and pepper. Beat together eggs and milk in shallow bowl until frothy. In electric frying pan or heavy, deep skillet, heat oil to 375°F. Add clarified butter. Roll fillets in flour mixture and shake off excess. Dip into egg white mixture, then coat with cornmeal mixture. Fry a few fingers at a time until deep golden brown and cooked through, about 2 minutes per side. Drain fish on paper towels; keep warm in oven while you fry remaining fish. Lightly splash with lemon juice and dust with your favorite seasoning.

4 to 6 servings.

Catfish Paprika Hungarian Style

$1/4$ cup butter ($1/2$ stick)
2 cups chopped onion
2 cloves garlic, minced
2 tsp. paprika
$1/2$ cup dry red wine
$1/2$ cup tomato purée
$1/4$ cup sliced pitted black olives ($1/4$-inch slices)
$1/4$ cup sliced mushrooms ($1/2$-inch slices)
1/2 cup chopped green pepper
1 tsp. salt
$1/4$ tsp. white pepper
4 cups catfish chunks (cut fillets into 2-inch chunks before measuring)
Sour cream and chopped fresh parsley for garnish
Fresh cooked homemade noodles

Heat oven to 350°F. In large skillet, heat butter over medium heat until melted and bubbling. Add onions and garlic; sauté until onions are tender. Blend in paprika. Add wine, tomato purée, olives, mushrooms, green pepper, salt, pepper and $1/3$ cup water. Heat to boiling. Reduce heat and simmer 10 minutes, stirring occasionally. Place catfish chunks in casserole dish; top with sauce. Cover and bake 30 minutes. Stir gently before serving. Garnish individual portions with sour cream and parsley; serve with fresh, homemade noodles sautéed in butter and poppy seeds.

4 to 6 servings.

Catfish and Morel Mushrooms.

Catfishing Strategies

Catfish and Morel Mushrooms

12 small to medium fresh
    morel mushrooms
1 cup all-purpose flour
1 tsp. salt
1/4 tsp. white pepper
4 catfish fillets
1/4 cup butter (1/2 stick)
1/4 cup white wine
1 T. lemon juice
2 tsp. finely minced fresh
    tarragon leaves

Wash and drain morels; pat dry with paper towels. Mix flour, salt and pepper in pie plate. Roll catfish fillets in flour mixture and shake off excess. In large skillet, heat butter over medium heat until melted and bubbling. Add fillets. Roll mushrooms quickly in flour and arrange around fillets in skillet. When fillets are lightly brown, turn fillets and mushrooms. Cook about 1 minute longer. Add white wine, lemon juice and tarragon. Reduce heat and simmer until fish flakes when probed with fork, about 3 minutes; do not overcook. Serve 3 mushrooms with each fillet.

4 servings.

Rack-Grilled Catfish

1 lb. catfish fillets, no thicker
    than 3/4 inch
1/4 cup butter or margarine (1/2
    stick)
Seasoned salt, or salt and pep-
    per

You will need 2 cake-cooling racks (approx. 10 x 14 inches), as well as 8 twist-ties from a box of sandwich bags (or substitute flexible wire for the twist-ties). Prepare charcoal grill. Butter top sides of each of the cake-cooling racks.

Arrange catfish fillets snugly on buttered side of one of the cake-cooling racks, placing any fillets that are thicker in center of rack. Thinner parts, like the rib area, can be overlapped slightly to fit all fillets on rack and to prevent overcooking of thin areas.

Place second rack, buttered-side down, on top of fillets. Wire long sides together tightly with twist-ties; if short ends are gapping, wire them together also. Melt butter in a small saucepan and keep hot. When coals are ready, place rack of fillets on grate. As soon as fillets are warmed by the fire, flip rack and brush butter over fillets, using a long-handled brush. When second side is warmed by the fire, flip and butter. Continue flipping and buttering frequently until fish flakes when probed with fork, about 10 minutes. To serve, cut twist-ties on one side and open racks like a book; season fillets with seasoned salt to taste.

3 servings.

Smoked Catfish

Brine mixture:
2 quarts water
1 cup canning/pickling salt
    (do not use iodized salt)
1 cup brown sugar
6 T. lemon juice or white wine
    vinegar
2 T. pickling spice, optional

Catfish fillets, preferably with
    skin on (dressed whole small
    catfish can also be used)
Damp wood chips for smoking
    (apple, cherry or other fruit
    wood is very good)

Combine brine mixture in non-metallic mixing bowl;

stir until salt is dissolved. Rinse catfish fillets and add to brine. Refrigerate 4 to 8 hours, depending on thickness. Thinner fillets should soak the shorter amount of time, while thicker fillets can soak as long as overnight. A longer soak produces a saltier, more flavorful product; experiment until you learn how you prefer your fish.

When soaking is complete, rinse fillets and pat dry with paper towels. Place on cake-cooling rack and allow to air-dry until surface of fish is smooth and shiny. You can direct a small fan over the fillets to hasten drying. While fillets are drying, pre-heat smoker as directed by the manufacturer (small electric smokers usually need about one-half hour pre-heating). Spray smoker racks with non-stick spray. Arrange dried fillets on racks without overlapping; leave some space between fillets to encourage air flow. Smoke at low temperature, 90° to 125°F, until fillets are done; this usually takes 5 to 8 hours, depending on thickness of fillets and weather conditions. When done, fish will seem firm and should flake when probed with a fork. Store smoked fish in the refrigerator; freeze for storage longer than 5 days.

Tip: For safety, many cooks raise the temperature of the smoker to 130°-140°F and hold it there for one-half hour after smoking time has been completed.

INDEX